No Time For Tears

This book shares the personal experiences and opinions of the author, who encountered and achieved near-complete recovery from Guillain Barré Syndrome. However, it is not designed to provide medical advice or guidance in the treatment of Guillain Barré Syndrome or any other health condition. As with any other serious medical condition, professional advice and treatment should be obtained from licensed physicians and therapists trained to diagnose and treat the condition. It is also advisable to consult a physician or qualified health care practitioner for any suspected health problem or before undertaking any type of supplemental nutritional program.

No Time For Tears
Turning Tragedy Into Triumph

Dorris R. Wilcox

With an appendix of resources for
patients with Guillain Barré Syndrome

SEA OATS
PRESS

Mt. Pleasant, S.C.

Publisher's Cataloging-in-Publication
(Provided by Quality Books, Inc.)

Wilcox, Dorris R.
No time for tears : transforming tragedy into triumph
/ by Dorris R. Wilcox. – 1st ed.
p. cm.
LCCN: 99-68983 ISBN: 1-929175-07-8

1. Wilcox, Dorris R.–Health. 2. Guillain-Barré
syndrome–Patients–United States–Biography. 3.
Self-care, Health. 4. Spiritual healing. 5. Wilcox,
Dorris R.–Religion.
I. Title.

RC416.W55A3 2000   362.1'9687
                          QB199-500559

Sea Oats Press

an imprint of

The Côté Literary Group
P.O. Box 1898
Mt. Pleasant, SC 29465 U.S.A.
(843) 881-6080
http://www.seaoatspress.com

Contents

Preface   ix
Acknowledgments   xii

Chapter One: Reaching for the Stars   1
Chapter Two: Knocked Flat!   20
Chapter Three: Led by Faith   40
Chapter Four: Breaking All the Rules   53
Chapter Five: Pushing Past the Limits   66
Chapter Six: Fighting for Freedom   88
Chapter Seven: God's Recovery Toolkit: 110
        Faith, Initiative and Action
Chapter Eight: Repaying the Gift   126
Appendix I: 149
    Sources for Guillain Barré Syndrome Information
    and Support
Appendix II: 157
    Internet Resources and Services Concerning
    Guillain Barré Syndrome
Appendix III: 161
    Publications about Guillain Barré Syndrome

For my sons, Michael H. Wilcox, Arthur W. Wilcox, and to my best friend, Betty Micheli.

Preface

If you don't know what you want, you won't get what you need.
— George Lowe

STOP IT NOW," I said to my family when the doctor opened the door and led them inside. "I'm not going to die. I'm too alive to die." The looks on their faces told me they believed the doctors instead of me. They were discouraged, and they'd made up their minds, but that only increased my strength and determination. I looked over at the neurosurgeon and waited for her to give her pronouncement.

Exactly one week after my flight back from a business trip to South Carolina and my first signs of fatigue and muscle aches, I found out just how badly those aches and pains had affected me. The doctors told me that I had Guillain Barré Syndrome — GBS — a rare neurological disorder. They told me that I might never walk again.

"You may never be able to take care of yourself," one of my brothers said.

"You guys need to lighten up," I said, glancing at their faces. "I'll be out of here in no time."

"You'll have to stay here for a while," the doctor said, clearing her throat. "You'll be sick for a long time, Dorris."

"I'm sorry honey," I said, "but we've got to do a whole lot better than that! I don't have that kind of time to be wasting in bed.

I've got a business to run!"

The neurosurgeon stared at me, blinked and said, "I'm sorry, Dorris, but this is something that you've got to deal with. Guillain Barré Syndrome is a very serious neurological disorder and you've been hit pretty hard. Your chances of regaining normal functions, such as walking and living independently, are . . . slim, at best."

"You don't know me. I will get better," I assured the doctor.

"All right, Dorris. If that's the way you want to feel, okay."

"Yes," I said, "that's how I want to feel: better. And I have no doubts at all that that's exactly how I'm going to feel. But you're the doctor and I need your help." The neurosurgeon furrowed her eyebrows and regarded me suspiciously. I knew she was trying to determine if I was kidding or if I was in denial about the prognosis she'd just made.

"Actually," I continued, "I need help from all the doctors. Now, I'm paralyzed at the moment, so could you go round up all the doctors who know anything about my case for me? I have a list of questions for them, and I want to understand everything thoroughly."

The doctor left without a word, having decided that I was neither kidding nor in denial, but rather that I was a "problem patient." And maybe I was, but the way I looked at it, problem-solving always requires a lot more work than peace.

This book describes the set of skills — which I call "God's Recovery Toolkit" — which I learned and developed through my eighteen-month ordeal after being struck with Guillain Barré Syndrome, a potentially lethal neurological disorder. Personal disasters of this magnitude happen to hundreds of thousands of people every year. I was knocked flat by GBS, but for another person, it could be a car accident or breast cancer that threatens their life and scrambles their assumptions, plans, and lifestyle. My story describes the course of a life that was satisfying and pleasantly predictable for sixty-one years — but turned ghastly and unbearable within a matter of days. The process I went through while learning how to successfully deal with my new realities taught me a lot about my own inner strength and the power of faith.

The result of my recovery process was the understanding of God's Recovery Toolkit: a combination of faith, innovation and perseverance in the face of adversity. As you read this story, you will find out how this medical emergency struck me down and how I persuaded and provoked my caregivers to speed my recovery. My faith in God, coupled with my willingness to become an expert on my own disease, facilitated my rapid recovery. This book is not about me, and it's not just about one person who was stricken with a particular rare disease. It's a guidebook, using my case as an example, designed to give advice, comfort and options to anyone faced with a life-changing disaster.

The contents of God's Recovery Toolkit can be used to deal with and solve almost any misfortune which strikes. My deepest aspiration in writing this book is that these tools will help you or someone you love find new hope, and, as I was able to, transform their own tragedy into triumph. Everything you read here is true. Only an occasional name has been changed for the sake of privacy.

Dorris R. Wilcox
January 3, 2000

Acknowledgments

I WOULD LIKE TO THANK the following people, who provided so much inspiration, help, and motivation during my recovery and while writing this book: my personal physician, Dr. John Blake; Dr. Jeffrey Hecht, Medical Director, Patricia Neal Rehabilitation Center; Dr. Winferd Holt; Darrell Monday of Ft. Sanders Regional Medical Center; Arthur P. Tranakis; and my friends at Home Federal Bank, Sevierville, Tennessee.

Finally, I'd like to extend my thanks to my literary collaborator and editor, Richard N. Côté, and to Dr. Elizabeth Burnett, Alicia Lutz, and Sarah Williams at Sea Oats Press for their invaluable assistance.

Chapter One:

Reaching for the Stars

I'D ALWAYS THRIVED ON ACTIVITY and spent my entire adult life creating a prosperous commercial design business. My business meant the world to me. It fed my appetite for an industrious and fast-paced lifestyle. Being busy didn't bother me, but wasting time sure did. When I was young, I could get mad with myself if I wasted five minutes. Back then, I couldn't even have imagined what it might be like to be kept from what I wanted to do for hours, weeks — or even years.

Efficiency and diligence were at the root of my upbringing. Keeping busy was one guideline that I never questioned. I was eleventh in a string of seven girls and seven boys, and whenever one person fell behind, the rest of the family pulled them up. Living on a farm in rural Dumpling Valley, Tennessee, meant we shared everything. To cover the two children who slept in each bed, my mother made quilts from cloth we received from our relatives.

My brothers chopped the wood that my sisters and I carried into the house. It was burned to warm the large farmhouse. From my father's cows, we got enough milk to help support the family. We raised chickens and pigs, and during the holidays we always had enough turkeys to feed Dumpling Valley.

Life could be difficult, but there was a basic sense to it. Mother managed our little operation and made sure we each knew what was expected of us. I learned early on that much more gets accomplished when everyone knows exactly which duties are required of them to help the unit as a whole. Looking back on it now, my childhood household was a business all on its own. In later life, it was clear that my tireless persistence and energetic determination to get a job done was something I learned in my childhood in Dumpling Valley.

Home was a strict environment for me. There were a lot of rules and regulations and, for the most part, I followed them. I managed to have fun, but between working on the farm and going to Midway Elementary School, I didn't have much free time. Even our social activities were scheduled. Once a year, for example, we went to visit our friends at their lake house in Athens, Tennessee. We'd frequently have family reunions where the whole family would come over to play horseshoes and have dinner. When the reunion was big enough, we'd also have family baseball games.

As I grew older and entered my teens, it didn't seem as much fun to spend all my free time with my family. I wanted to meet more people my age. Going to Carter High School every day just didn't generate enough social interaction anymore. My brothers and sisters and I started meeting our neighbors for socials. It was usually just a day of silly games, such as guessing who is talking to you while you're blindfolded, but getting away from the farm was great.

My mother trained all fourteen of us to be church-goers, and even though we were members of a small Methodist church, we attended many different churches and church events. When I was at the "boy-crazy" age of fifteen or sixteen, my favorite events were the box suppers. The girls carried boxes with dinners in them and the boys bid on whichever girl they thought was cute. Of course they weren't really bidding on the girls — they were bidding on the dinner in the girl's box. Everyone knew what a great cook my mother was, so I always had the highest bids: about seven or eight dollars, which was a high price for a boxed dinner at that time.

I attribute my intolerance for idleness to my family. I cannot recall one lull in my life, not one period in time in which I dawdled or dallied. At age seventeen I realized that I wasn't going to make any money, or meet or learn anything new if I stayed on the farm. In an effort to better myself, and in accordance with the trend at the time, I decided to go to "the big city" — Knoxville — to find both my own way and a job doing something I'd enjoy.

"I'm going to put my hair up on my head and I'll look so good, all the boys will ask me out," I remember telling my sister. "Plus, I'll look nineteen, and then I'll have a better chance of being hired."

I lived out on the farm at first, but moved in with my aunt in Knoxville after a short while. I got a job, but I don't think it was because the people at Rohm Haas thought I was nineteen! They needed an inspector to make sure the Plexiglas windows for airplanes didn't have any bubbles or defects, and they didn't care how old I was. I worked at the glass plant for three years. I went in to get my paycheck one day in my third year and overheard a couple of the other employees talking about going to Detroit. I'd been itching to get to Detroit for some time. I knew a lot of people from Knoxville who had moved to Detroit for work, and everything I'd heard about it sounded wonderfully exciting. I got a wild idea.

"If y'all are going to Detroit for the weekend, I believe I'll go too."

As it turns out, the girl and her boyfriend who were going obviously didn't want me tagging along. But I went anyway, and seven hours later, I was in Detroit. The couple dropped me off to stay with some family friends of mine.

I really hadn't planned on staying in Detroit, but it was just too exciting to leave. I spent the first two weeks learning about the city — especially how to get around on the buses and street-cars — and getting in touch with friends living there. Once I'd mastered the art of getting to where I wanted to go in that foreign place, I began the job hunt. The work I'd done at Rohm Haas had given me plenty of experience in inspecting airplane parts, and I landed a job Bower Roller Bearings in no time.

As soon as I got the job, I returned to the farm to collect all my things.

"Aren't you scared?" my younger brother, J. D., asked me when I told him my plans.

"No," I said. "I'm excited."

"That's her problem," my father said frankly. "She's never been scared in her life."

He was right. Although I was a bit overwhelmed by Detroit and my move there, I was never scared. It was more like waking up and having a whole new world to experience. Everything was faster and more exciting than in Knoxville, and the days always flew by, unlike anything I was accustomed to. There were all sorts of differences, of course. The "city people" were different. They seemed distant and withdrawn in comparison to the people I'd always passed on sidewalks back home. There was a general at-titude of, "I'm in a hurry! I'm late! No time now!" It was an atti-tude I thrived on, and I fell into the lifestyle of a city girl very easily.

In 1954, four years after I'd first come to Detroit, four girls I'd met at work and I went dancing at a club. I was having a won-derful time, when I barely heard, "I believe I've seen you some-where before."

I turned in the direction of the low voice to see a tall, dark and handsome Naval cadet with the prettiest long eyelashes. I was sure I'd remember that face if I'd seen it before. "Oh come on," I said, accusing him of using the same old line as all the others.

"No," he said. "I believe I've seen you." He looked at my face like he was trying to remember and then, after a few seconds, he introduced himself as Bill and asked me to dance. We'd only been dancing for a minute when he pulled back a little bit to look at my face again. "Where are you from originally?" he asked.

"Tennessee," I told him.

"Where in Tennessee?"

"Knoxville area," I said.

He smiled a little bit and nodded his head. "Do you remember — oh, I guess about four years ago — meeting a cadet named Bill?"

I thought back to four years ago when all the cadets came to the university in Knoxville to train for the Korean War. "Of course!" I exclaimed, suddenly remembering Bill. "What do you know! So that wasn't just a come-on!"

We had made small talk every time we saw each other out at clubs, and here we were dancing in Detroit. It turns out Bill had recently been stationed here and he didn't know much about the city. So, over the next eight months, he and I got to know each other as he grew familiar with the place.

He was from New York City, which made it interesting for me to spend so much time with him because our backgrounds were so different. He always referred to stores, movies, and famous people whom I'd never even heard of. "Remember, Bill," I'd say, "I'm a country girl."

"I don't think of you as a country girl," he said. "I think of you as someone who has a bright future and lots of things just waiting to happen. You're an entrepreneur who just hasn't had the chance to try out all your ideas."

My parents, however, still thought of me as a country girl. When Bill asked my father for my hand in marriage, it was clear that they did not want me marrying a city boy. I think they liked *him*; they just didn't like the fact that he was from New York.

Undeniably, I was going to do whatever I wanted to do, and my parents recognized that, so Bill and I married. The little girl from Dumpling Valley was now the wife of a New York-born U.S. Navy officer.

He proved to be the perfect husband for me. A real handyman. He could do almost anything he wanted to: carpentry work, cooking — and he was even a good shopper! He was very proud, and he wanted to make sure that I looked good at all times, so he'd sometimes surprise me with smart new outfits. I'd never known a man who knew how to pick out clothes so well for a woman, and I've never met one since!

Not long after we were married, I found out that I had a uterine cyst which would prevent me from having children. The condition was in direct conflict with my whole concept of family life. I consulted my doctor, protesting, "But I want children! What can I do?"

"Well," he said, "you could always adopt."

I thought about it and discussed it with Bill, who immediately became excited about the idea. But we'd both gotten too excited a little too soon. One complication after another kept us from adopting the little boy we wanted. Finally, in 1954, almost eighteen months after his birth, we received Arthur William Wilcox as our adoptive son. As all proud parents do, we fell in love with him.

"Isn't he wonderful?" I said to Bill after we'd tucked him into bed that first night.

"He sure is," Bill replied. "But it's you that amazes me. I don't think anything can keep you from getting what you want."

It may have been Bill's faith in me that inspired me to venture out a little bit. I was satisfied with my job at Bower Roller Bearings and I stayed with them for many more years, but I wanted to move. I'd always loved the spectacular houses in Grosse Pointe, Michigan, and longed for the day when I could live in one. I started brainstorming on ways we could live there with the budget we were on. It wasn't long before I'd come up with a solution.

"Bill," I said, "I'm going to go down the street and talk to a realtor, Allen Marcus, to see if we can't rent one of those big houses down there at Grosse Pointe."

"Okay," Bill said. "Where are you getting the money?" He knew me well enough to know I already had a plan.

"I was thinking we could rent some of the rooms out to people — to our friends," I said. "That should pay for it. What do you think?"

"You really know how to get what you want, don't you?" he smiled.

I rented a beautiful fifteen-room home in Grosse Pointe, my first move toward what was to become an invigorating and prosperous career. Ever since high school I'd been interested in design. I loved math, home economics and sewing, but it was the pictures in my history book that fascinated me. Looking at the photographs of different parts of the world, the architecture and decorations, always struck me. I think it was then that I knew in my heart that travel would be an integral part of my life. I wanted to explore and visit all those beautiful castles and museums. At that point, I became interested in fixing up houses as well. Once I knew how beautiful a building could look, I wanted to make them all exquisite.

We didn't really have the means to make the house look like Palacio Real or anything, but Bill and I fitted it out with nice beds, furniture, and decorations. There were many changes I wanted to make, and Bill was always willing to help. Plus, he had the know-how.

"I think this room should have a window," I'd say to him.

"I don't, but if that's what you want. . . ." And pretty soon the room would have a window, or a door, or whatever I wanted it to have. Even if Bill didn't think what I was proposing would look good, he was always willing to do the work — and he was always impressed with the results.

"How do you do that?" he'd ask me. "How do you know what'll look good before you've even seen it?"

As soon as the house was ready for its boarders, my business took off. I had a lot of friends living in the area, many of whom agreed to move into the house and pay room and board. My nephew and brother even paid to live there when they got jobs in Detroit.

Since I was still working at Bower Roller Bearings, it wasn't long before I had a chunk of money and I knew exactly what I wanted to do with it: buy, renovate and resell houses. The taste of interior design that the boarding house project had given me was all it took. I wanted to restore homes to make them look the best they possibly could.

I bought houses all over Detroit, mainly in Grosse Pointe, as cheaply as possible, and then I'd spend a year or so renovating them for resale — a tempting endeavor indeed, but not an easy task for the average entrepreneur. In order to keep from losing a lot of money in such a business, I had to pay close attention to every detail and work very hard. Fortunately, that's just what I'd learned from my family while growing up in Dumpling Valley.

By whatever means, I gained quite a reputation through this little indulgence, earning me the nickname "Mrs. Grosse Pointe."

In 1960, two years after I'd first rented the boarding house, I began considering giving it up and concentrating on my renovations and my job at Bower Roller Bearings. The decision was made for me, however, when I went to look at a huge, beautiful house on the lake that had just become available. When the owner of the house agreed to sell it to me with $250 down, I jumped at the opportunity.

Two years later, the Navy transferred Bill to Virginia Beach, Virginia. After that we began to move often, as Navy personnel and their families are prone to do. Though the constant relocation made it hard to secure a business, I did manage to study interior design at the Chicago School of Design while Bill was stationed at the Great Lakes Naval Air Station.

Not long after I graduated, Bill was transferred to the Charleston Navy Base in South Carolina. He told me that we were going to stay in one place for a while, and so I knew it was time to get serious about launching my career. I opened not one, but two shops: Southern Seat Covering Company, in north Charleston, and Demoor's Awning Company. Later, I also opened a design shop in nearby Mt. Pleasant and an antique store in the heart of downtown Charleston.

I enjoyed running my businesses and was delighted to finally be settled. It felt good to have a home and a family that I could call my own. Bill, Arthur, and I spent long summer evenings at the beaches in the area, and I was starting to realize that this was only the beginning of a wonderful life together.

I'd come to know Jan Easton through some interior design classes I was involved in at the College of Charleston. She and I were good friends, and she always said that I was like a mother to her. "Only there are some things I can't tell my mother," she said quietly one afternoon.

"Like what?" I asked.

"Oh, Dorris, I don't know what to do," she sighed. "I'm pregnant."

I didn't know what to do either, but I tried to be as helpful as possible by finding her an obstetrician. Shortly thereafter, I invited her to come live with Arthur and me. Bill had been sent to Italy in 1964.

"I've got a huge house," I told her. "There's plenty of room. Come stay with us. You can be part of our family."

Jan ended up contributing more a part of our family than I'd ever expected. And I simply couldn't resist it when, one morning, she came downstairs with her big round belly, and said, her tone saturated with emotion, "Dorris, I want you to adopt my baby. I want you to be its mama."

I melted. I wanted to help her and I wanted another child, but

I knew better than to make any promises before I'd discussed it with Bill and Arthur to see how they felt about an addition to the family.

"Well, Honey, we'll see," Bill said when he called and I posed the idea. "I'd love to — I want whatever you do — but I just don't know when I'll be back."

The baby didn't care whether Bill was in Charleston or not. Time was running out and I kept remembering how long it'd taken to go through the adoption process for Arthur. I didn't want Jan's baby to suffer the confusion that Arthur had. Bill had given me his power of attorney early on in our marriage, and I decided to go ahead and get an attorney and start the process without him.

"I just didn't know if you'd be back in time," I told him when he called again.

"I wish I could be there," he said wistfully, but I could tell he was happy.

Arthur was ecstatic about having someone to play with. "Hurry up, slow-poke," he'd tell the baby in Jan's stomach.

The baby, of course, was no slow-poke. In fact, I was constantly wishing we could delay the delivery for Bill's return. But then one night, six months after he'd left, the phone rang and it was Bill.

"I'll be home tomorrow," he said, his elation practically brimming over the phone line. "Pick me up at 4:40 P.M."

Well, at 4:00 P.M. the next day, Jan went into labor. I ran her to the hospital and then dashed off to the airport.

"We have to go to the hospital," I announced once we were in the car.

"What? Why?"

"Our child will be here soon," I said.

He almost ran the car off the road, and then cried, "Dear God! What are we going to do?"

"We're going to have a child," I said. "I've taken care of

everything. If it's a girl we'll call her Darla and if it's a boy will call him Michael."

He stared at me while we sat at an intersection. "You're something else," he said.

"Never give a lady your power of attorney before you leave the country," I grinned. "You might end up with twins."

But, much to Bill's relief, only one baby — Michael Hugo Wilcox — was born the next morning.

In 1967, I decided I was ready to buy another business. My industrious character aided in the success of most of my projects, even if it was what had always been considered "man's work."

I bought the Southern Seat Covering Company, which specialized in restoring vintage automobile headliners, door panels, and carpets to their original condition. One of the first jobs I took on was the restoration of an antique Mercedes Benz. The owner of the car was so impressed with my work that when he later bought a World War II underground ammunition magazine and turned it into a house, he asked me to do the designing. In addition, I restored a baby grand piano, and designed his window treatments and upholstered furniture for him.

Although I loved the process of restoration, Southern Seat Covering focused more on repair than on renovation, and, after a while, I found my love of design being suppressed. I bought Demore's Awning and Tent Company, where I could better implement my design skills. I paid the former owner, who had been in the awning business for thirty years, to tell me what to do. Before long, I was renovating twenty ships at a time as the designer for Braswell & Detyens's Shipyard. I was delighted with the rapid pace and the intensity of the projects, and I relished the activity that surrounded me. The whirlwind of work was where I always wanted to be, and right in the center.

In fact, even though I was always working with my two companies and running my shops, I still couldn't get enough of the action. I became set on finding something more and, about a year after I'd bought Southern Seat Company, I began doing design work for the Westvaco Corporation, an international paper manufacturer. But I wasn't designing paper.

Using my skills from the awning company, I designed the covers for the big trucks that carry huge rolls of newsprint and corrugated paper across the nation. Until then, the covers had been made of canvas, and had a tendency to flap around and leak, rendering the paper products worthless. However, I fixed that by making them out of Herculon and Faclon, and by securing the flaps with grommets to keep the water from getting in. My work was never done, but my confidence in my accomplishments grew as my solutions to corporate problems proved to be rewarding, lucrative and effective.

Work? I couldn't get enough of it. I remember telling Bill that I wanted to redesign the interior of all the ships of the U.S. Navy's Sixth Fleet, then headquartered at the Charleston Navy Base in North Charleston. There seemed to be about ten of them there.

He looked at me as if I'd gone crazy. "The whole Sixth Fleet? Do you know how many ships there are in the U.S. Sixth Fleet?"

"Sure I do, honey," I said. "Why not?"

"Aren't you busy enough as it is, Dorris?"

"I'm never busy enough," I laughed. "You know that."

"You're crazy," he said with a shrug. He knew he couldn't stop me from inquiring about redecorating the fleet. And he didn't try.

Five days later, after explaining my course of action and the logistics behind it, I signed a contract that specified the arrangement under which I was to redecorate all the submarines, carriers, and frigates in the entire Sixth Fleet.

Anticipating working on a maximum of ten ships, I was

shocked when I understood the reality of the situation. Now I knew why my husband had asked me if I knew what I was doing. The ten ships in port when I counted them were just the ones that weren't at sea at that time. I was now in charge of refurnishing, carpeting, painting, and decorating ninety ships!

My husband was flabbergasted when I told him the news, but I was ecstatic. It was an interior designer's dream come true — from the draperies in the officers' quarters to the murals in the dining halls, I was in charge of making everything look its best.

It was the biggest project I'd ever been given, and I couldn't have enjoyed it more. The unlimited possibilities coupled with the vast responsibilities that the project offered me were both exhilarating and inspiring. And though I never sought a job quite that big again, the size and complexity of that project convinced me I could do anything I set my mind to.

While I was working on the fleet, I also managed to buy and restore a house on beautiful Sullivan's Island, South Carolina, a few miles from Charleston. As we walked through the house, the realtor told me the sad, depressing story of the former owner, who had been stricken with polio on her wedding day, never to walk again. I pitied her, but I could hardly fathom her unfortunate situation and how devastating it must have been for her and her husband. Three years and forty gallons of paint later, I had completed the renovation, sold it, and completely forgotten the tragic story of the lady with polio.

Soon enough, I was to learn for myself what it's like when illness surprises you, flips over your life, and destroys life as you know it — even before you know what's hit you.

Not long after I had completed the Sixth Fleet at the Charleston Naval Base, I began winning scores of military contracts for interior design — on cruisers, freighters, mine sweepers, airplanes, theaters, training centers, officers' quarters and clubs in various states. I had finally earned a national reputation in interior design and, though most would be satisfied with that, I knew my career had only just begun.

One day in October of 1974, while standing on a ladder putting up the cornice boards in the house I was renovating, the telephone rang.

"Will you get that?" I called to one of the men working with me.

He immediately brought the phone to me. "Said it's an emergency," he reported with a curious look on his face.

I came down a few steps so that the cord would reach and took the phone from him. "Hello?"

"Dorris, it's Bill. Do you not know what's going on?"

"I beg your pardon?"

"I was coming home from the Navy shipyard and passed by our house," he said quickly. "It caught fire."

"Oh my goodness," I replied, steadying myself on the ladder.

"I'm coming to get you," he said. "Just leave your car parked there, I'm going to pick you up."

Bill drove me back to Sullivan's Island and my heart was pounding as we pulled up to the house. I didn't know if I'd be able to handle this kind of sudden and dreadful catastrophe.

Another car pulled up just as we did. A neighbor apparently hadn't known where anyone was. Figuring Michael would be at Porter-Gaud School, he went and got him. As soon as the car stopped, Michael jumped out and came running into my arms.

"What's going to happen?" he asked, tears streaming down his face.

"I don't know, Michael," I said, shaking my head. "I just don't know."

The fire, it turned out, had begun with an electrical short in the furnace. By the time it was over, ninety-seven percent of the house had been destroyed. My family and I were left with no place to live. For the first time in my life, I felt defeated by stress and depression. Never before had I been faced with such a situation and I saw no way to make anything good out of it.

However, I remembered a time when I was lost and lacking direction. I was nine years old, sitting in church with my family, when God came into my heart and saved me by dissipating my feelings of loss. That memory renewed my faith in believing I could pull through. For without faith, we have nothing. Nothing at all.

With my revitalized faith and the help of some wonderful people, I was able to get back on my feet. As soon as my sisters in Knoxville learned what had happened, they went shopping together and bought me an entire wardrobe. Mr. J. C. Long, who was known on the Isle of Palms for providing low-cost housing to veterans returning from World War II, opened up three side-by-side apartments for us.

"Dorris, just don't get upset now," he told me. "Take your time, and we can go over there later to see what needs to be done."

Absolutely everything needed to be done. Seeing all of our things completely destroyed nearly broke my heart.

"At least your rose garden is okay," Michael pointed out when we went to look at the house.

I smiled. That garden was very special to me. Bill had bought each of those roses individually for various occasions. He planted each one of them, and I'd eventually ended up with a whole bed of roses. "So you can look at them and you'll see how much you mean to me," he had told me.

It took a long time for the inspectors to do the investigation, and we had to stay in the unit that Mr. Long provided for three months before we could move back into the house. I'd decided to renovate what was left of the house and to add a third floor, and though we had to live in the downstairs for a year and a half, we survived. I don't know how, but we survived.

I was always busy balancing all my work. Bill was teaching at the Navy base, Michael was going to school, and Arthur had moved out and was working in Mt. Pleasant. Everything went along smoothly for two years. Everything, that is, until 1976 when my husband died. If I'd ever felt really lost, it was then. I didn't know which way to go or what to do.

Fortunately, the Navy gave me legal help and most of the answers I needed. The only question they couldn't answer was, "What now?" It was more than money, property and insurance. It was my wonderful husband, my soulmate, my cheerleader, my support, and he was gone.

The only solution I knew was to keep myself busy. I still had my shops and my companies and I was still decorating clubs, churches, factories, federal buildings and yacht clubs. So, when a friend of mine who was associated with Trident Technical College in North Charleston mentioned that the school was looking for an instructor in interior design for Continuing Education students, I enthusiastically grabbed the opportunity.

I've always been convinced that real experience is better than book learning, and that principle drove the way I conducted my classes. We traveled the Low Country to see different examples of design. The only days that we were actually in the classroom were exam days and roundtable days, when we sat around and discussed design techniques and styles.

I taught for two years, and I'll never forget my students. It is a wonderful thing to watch the faces of young people as they realize the same wonders that we've been taking for granted for so long. I wanted my students see things they'd never noticed before. Once their eyes were opened, they could see a whole new beauty in the world, a whole new glow, and all I wanted them to do was embrace it.

I accomplished a lot in the twenty-one years that I lived in Charleston, where I had begun my career, raised a family, and established a reputation for myself. However, in 1982, I felt like it was time to leave. I sold my holdings in South Carolina and moved back to Tennessee, but I always carried Charleston with me, even naming my new business in Knoxville "Charleston Interiors."

Three years later, though my business was prosperous, I opened Pharaoh Design in West Knoxville, through which I started doing a lot of larger jobs again. One of those jobs involved design work for the University of Tennessee in Knoxville. Upon completion, they were so pleased with my work that they hired me to teach interior design.

I loved my work and I loved all the people I met. I was having the time of my life with my business and I was staying very busy, but after a while I realized that I couldn't do it all by myself anymore. I was doing a lot of traveling and, while I was still working on state and federal buildings, I had begun scoring some big commercial contracts for hotels and motels all over the world. It was time for me to hire additional designers.

By January of 1989, I had nine designers and twenty-five other regular employees, including wallpaper hangers and carpet layers. My big projects often required up to seventy-five laborers. When I did those jobs, I would hire workers through the state unemployment office to do things such as set up beds, hang mirrors and install televisions. I became accustomed to taking control of large work groups. I guess I'd inherited some of my mother's managerial skills, because I came to love giving orders and having people follow my directions. As a manager, I was truly in my element.

The process of renovating a hotel may have been my favorite out of all the projects I'd done. After setting up my headquarters in one room, my crew and I would formulate our plan of attack, refurbishing one side of the establishment at a time to prevent having to shut it down altogether. Typically, we gutted each room and started from scratch. It was in this type of project that you could really see the progress as you went along, and that was an amazing feeling. You'd look at it when you were done and then think back to how it had looked without any carpet or any countertops or anything, and you'd say, "So that's why I haven't had time to sleep for ten months!"

There is nothing which can match the sense of achievement you get when you complete a job that you started from scratch. The satisfaction that follows is much more rewarding, no matter how extensive the planning that goes into such a renovation.

As time went on, more rewarding jobs came my way. My business was flourishing and, when I was commissioned to renovate two large hotels in South Carolina — in Beaufort and Hilton Head Island — for a total of a million dollars, I felt my career was in its heyday.

After a week of preparing proposals for these jobs, I took a two-day trip to South Carolina and presented my prospective approach and its cost to the owner of the two hotels. The job at the Hilton Hotel on Hilton Head involved the renovation of over 100 rooms. The Great Oaks in Beaufort had 300 rooms, fifteen-foot-wide halls, a bar, lawn and swimming pool that needed to be completely restored. I explained to the owner what I planned to do and showed him samples of the wallpaper, carpeting, drapery and bedspreads that I had selected for the establishments. I also offered pictures of the furniture and the artwork that I suggested.

After four hours of presentation at Great Oaks, not only had I secured a contract with them, but I had also been beseeched to give presentations at the Ramada and Hampton Inns in town. I conducted another full presentation to these two hotels, leaving them with material to look over and I took off for the Charleston airport to catch my flight back home.

As I approached the airport, I remember feeling as if I were further from home than I'd ever been before: a very odd sensation considering not only that I had lived in the Charleston area for twenty-one years, but also that I'd recently been abroad.

Still, I ached to be resting, undisturbed, in the comfort of my own bed. Little did I know, however, I'd soon be stuck in bed, redefining "aching" for myself and longing to move once again.

Chapter Two:
Knocked Flat!

B<small>Y THE TIME I ARRIVED IN ATLANTA</small>, I had a pretty good idea that what I was feeling was more than exhaustion: I was coming down with the flu. My entire body was sore, and my legs and feet throbbed with severe pain. I couldn't imagine how I'd gotten so sick so quickly. I hadn't done anything strenuous or dangerous in South Carolina, and I was generally healthy.

Of all times to get sick, I thought as I boarded the plane for Knoxville. *Well, at least I'm going home; at least it didn't hit me on Sunday.* I was leaving Sunday night for another presentation in Albuquerque, New Mexico and, since I hadn't fully prepared the presentation, I urgently needed rest so I could handle all my responsibilities there.

I was sitting next to a young girl from Atlanta and, in the middle of our conversation about the renovations she wanted to make on her house, she interrupted to ask me if I was all right.

"You don't look well," she said. "You're pale."

"I am a little chilly," I told her.

She touched my hand and looked at me with wide eyes. "Your hands are as cold as ice!"

The aching was growing worse by the minute and I was growing increasingly more worried. I told the flight attendant that I wasn't feeling good, and she told the pilot. They seemed concerned and wanted to know if I would be okay to drive home from the airport. I assured them that I was fine and I promised to rest a bit before getting on the road.

But my anxiety increased — not so much about my condition as about my work. *I can't get sick,* I told myself as I hurried off the plane in Knoxville. *I've got too much to do!*

Because I wanted to nip this thing in the bud, I decided to stop off at the University of Tennessee Hospital to talk to a doctor I knew there. Upon informing him of my muscle aches and lack of energy, he confirmed my suspicion; it was probably the flu and I should go home and get some rest. On my way out of the hospital, I called Dr. John Blake, my family physician. He wasn't in the office, but I talked to his secretary, Mary. I told her I'd call back if I felt any worse and she promised to tell Dr. Blake I'd called.

By now, I ached all over. Everything hurt, and I was exhausted. It took just about all I had to drive home. I stopped five times along the side of the road to rest and pull my energy together. Finally, I made it to my front door.

I lived above my shop. Out of habit, I went straight to the answering machine and listened to my messages. The machine was completely full, and the more I listened, the more determined I became to beat whatever it was that was draining me of energy.

On top of all the other projects I already had underway, the Ramada and the Hampton Inns, with whom I'd met earlier that day, had already sent telegrams to confirm the contracts I had proposed to them. All of a sudden, the magnitude of all of the jobs that I had in front of me was overwhelming. I had always been able to handle everything and I usually strove for more, but just thinking about all the things I had to do made me tired and weak.

As my worry continued to grow, I called my younger sister, Naomi, and told her I'd arrived safely home, but that I was sick.

"Come stay with me," she said. "You can rest here until you feel better."

"I don't know," I said. "I don't feel like driving, and besides...."

"Come on, Dorris," she said. "I'll see you soon."

I packed a bag, took an antihistamine, and got into my car. Naomi lives in Kodak, which is about fifteen minutes away from where I was living, but that fifteen minutes seemed like an eternity. When I finally got to her house, it was all I could do to force myself to her front door.

"You look as pale as death," Naomi said, her concern showing as she helped me inside.

"You'll have to get my stuff for me," I said weakly. I'd never known it took so much energy to talk! My entire body ached and had the sensation of being internally attacked. "I've got to lie down. I'm exhausted from the trip."

Naomi turned down the bed for me and tried to feed me some soup, but I couldn't eat. I took another decongestant and fell asleep, hoping I would feel better in the morning.

Instead of feeling better when I awoke, however, I felt much, much worse. Nevertheless, I was determined to go home and tend to my business. I needed to pack my bags for Albuquerque and go to the laundromat. Even though my body was getting weaker, my determination was as strong as ever, and I put forth all my effort to force my way through the day and accomplish what needed to be done.

As soon as I left my sister's house, I started feeling nauseous. I'm still not sure how I made it to the laundromat, but I insisted on having my clothes washed for my business trip. While I was doing laundry, the most horrific pains shot through my arms, legs, and neck, making me so queasy that I had to lie down.

A friend of mine came in just as my clothes were finishing, and he seemed very worried about me. I told him I was fine, but he didn't look convinced and insisted on taking my clothes out of the dryer and carrying them to the car.

The rest of the day flew by in a blur. My energy continued to plummet, the aching advanced in intensity, and my listlessness grew by the minute. I kept taking the sinus medication, making me even drowsier. All I could do was sleep.

When I woke up Saturday I didn't feel any better. My energy was tapped out and I felt faint. I got back in bed for a while, but the responsibilities of work would not let me rest. The phone was ringing off the hook and I couldn't stand to let it go unanswered. I spent the majority of the day trying to pack for my trip, but that simple task now seemed more daunting than any I'd ever imagined.

I somehow managed to get two bags together with all my clothes, toiletries, presentational material, and paperwork. At that point, I was forced to call it a day. I phoned my sisters and my designers, telling them not to call for the rest of the evening. "I simply don't have the energy to talk with anyone," I told them. "I'm not well and I need to rest up for my trip tomorrow."

My designers were shocked. They had always known me as the one always ready to talk about our projects; the woman who was never tired of working. But I had no energy whatsoever, and was beginning to realize that I was pretty sick. Nothing had ever kept me from my activities before, and here I was, too tired to talk on the phone!

It troubled me that I was so ill, and I couldn't help but wonder what was happening to me. I got in bed around nine that night and speculated about the possibilities of my condition. It has to be some kind of awful flu that won't be so awful by morning, I reassured myself.

On Sunday morning I got up to get dressed for church. I remember having the strangest sensation, a feeling that I had never experienced before: I just didn't feel like doing anything. It was like I was caught up in this lethargic inertia or malaise. I didn't feel like myself at all, that's for sure. *What in the world is wrong with me?* I wondered. *I've never had a flu like this!*

Hoping a cup of coffee would help, I worked my way down to the kitchen to make some. As I made my way down the stairs, my legs began to quiver, as if they were made of jelly or sponge. I couldn't imagine what was wrong with me. By the time I got to the kitchen door, the room was spinning.

Suddenly, I fainted, hitting my head on the wall and falling flat onto the floor.

When I came to, two hours later, I was lying on the floor, drenched with perspiration. It was like somebody had dipped me in the bathtub without my knowing it. I tried to get up, but I couldn't budge. I lay there, in a pool of sweat, struggling to move and thinking, *Oh, no! I've broken my hip! What am I going to do?*

I needed help. With some effort, I managed to push and scoot myself across the floor and over to the counter. I reached for the telephone cord, pulled the phone off the counter and slid it over in my direction. I don't remember thinking about who to call, or if I should call 911 first, or anything. I just grabbed the phone and dialed one of my designer's numbers. In a very calm voice, I told her that I had fallen, that I had cut my eye and my head, and that I couldn't walk.

"God! No!" she cried.

"Now, hold on. Calm down," I said. "Do you have a key to the front door of the shop?" She said that she did. "Could you get someone else to come, too?" I asked. "It's going to take two of you to move me."

"Yes, of course," she said. "I'll be right there,"

"Now wait," I said. "You two go to church first and then come get me, okay?"

I'd barely gotten those words out of my mouth when my designer and Janna, the woman who ran my shop, arrived. Seeing the cut on my head, they frantically helped me up to get me to the hospital for stitches.

"Hold on a minute," I told them. "There are some things I've got to do before we leave. I can't go anywhere until I clean up.

And I need a bath. I want to be clean and dressed nice before I go."

But they wouldn't hear anything of it.

"Okay, then I'd like to rest in a chair for a minute."

"Oh, no," Janna said. "You might never get out of it. We're taking you to the hospital now."

They called Dr. Blake and, after telling him to meet us at Fort Sanders Regional Hospital, they made a packsaddle to use for carrying me out to the car. Before I knew what was happening, they had whisked me from home and to the hospital.

Dr. Blake had been getting ready for church when Janna had called, and he was wearing his necktie when he met me at the hospital. He wanted to know where my pain was concentrated, but I was aching everywhere.

"It feels like it does when someone twists your arm, but all over," I told him. "In the back of my neck, in my legs. I've got a throbbing headache and there's constant pain in my arms. And I'm positively sure my hip is broken."

As soon as I'd said that, a shadow fell across Dr. Blake's face, and he rushed me in for an X-ray.

When he had returned with the results, his forehead was wrinkled, making him look very worried. "Why did you think your hip was broken, Dorris?" he asked.

"Because I fell and when I tried to get up, I couldn't," I said. "I can't walk."

"Well, you have no broken bones," Dr. Blake said. "Your glasses are broken, and the cut on your head needs stitching, but no broken bones. How are you feeling now?"

"Everything's hurting," I said. "Even my fingernails."

He nodded and did a reflex test on my knee. Nothing happened.

I stared at him. "What's wrong with my reflexes?"

"Well," he said after a minute, "putting together your symptoms and the fact that you don't have any broken bones, I'm thinking there might be something wrong with your nervous system. The thing is, with your symptoms, it's hard to determine the proper diagnosis. Don't worry, though, we'll figure it out. We should see a pattern in your symptoms. Can you answer some questions for me?"

I nodded even though I didn't feel much like talking at all. However, I managed to answer all the questions thoroughly. He wanted to know about the trip abroad I'd recently taken and about what kind of shots I'd had before I left. He listened carefully as I struggled to tell him everything I could remember.

"Dorris," Dr. Blake said, "how did this come on? Did you hurt on both sides of your body, or did you notice it on one side of your body first?"

"It all came on at once," I said. "First my feet and then my legs and my hips and my back."

"Uh-huh," Dr. Blake muttered. He rolled his pen between his index finger and his thumb for a second. "And when did you first notice it?"

"Thursday," I said.

"So your muscles weakened in a matter of three days, then. Right?"

"Yes, that's right," I said. I didn't know what any of this meant, of course, and I had no way of knowing how obvious the problem was becoming to Dr. Blake. My answers to his questions were the typical diagnostic responses for a debilitating nerve condition called Guillain Barré Syndrome (GBS).

"I've got an idea about what's going on, Dorris," Dr. Blake said after a while. "But I want to make sure. I don't want to misdiagnose."

I asked him what he thought it was, and he told me not to get too worried yet, but it sounded like a pretty serious condition that is hard to overcome. "If that's what it is, you can expect to get worse before you get better," he informed me.

"Oh, no," I said. "That's not it, then. I can't have that. I have a lot of work right now, and tourist season is coming up." I almost felt relieved that it wasn't pneumonia or something like that; I could get pneumonia, but I knew I couldn't have anything serious.

"Well, we'll see," he said. "We've got some investigating to do."

"What kind of investigating?" I asked. The word investigating struck me as having a particularly slow and long-term quality to it, which was not what I wanted to hear. I wanted to know what was wrong and how to fix it.

"Well, that depends on how the first few tests go," he said. "If we can be sure of what's going on with a simple muscle-strength test, or a perception or sensation test, then that's it. This kind of condition affects people in all sorts of ways, and the response to testing is really dependent on the individual case. Plus, there are a lot of disorders of the nervous system that share symptoms, so we have to be careful not to jump to any conclusions. I'll tell you all about the other diagnostic tests we have if we decide you need something else. There's no point in confusing you with that right now."

"Don't worry," I replied simply. "You won't have to go through it with me anyway because I don't have anything like what you're talking about. Let's get these tests started so I can get back to business."

There were several doctors examining me, but it was Dr. Blake who directed the exhaustive battery of testing. The doctors wanted to see what happened when I tried to walk or stand. They took me out into the hallway, watching and scribbling in notebooks as I flopped immediately to the floor.

"Oh Lord," I heard one doctor say to another. Although he was talking under his breath, I overheard him. "I hope she doesn't have what I think she has. She's got the symptoms."

I still had no idea what they were referring to, but I was sure that, whatever it was, I couldn't have it. I didn't think twice that the doctors' suspicions were right. *I'll show them,* I remember thinking.

By 1:30 that afternoon, however, the paralysis had progressed and I was moved into a room by myself. Still thinking I'd be released that day, I tried to convince Dr. Blake that I didn't need a room, but he insisted.

"The tests gave us some more clues as to what we're dealing with, Dorris," he said. "And through the process of elimination, there are fewer and fewer diagnoses we can conclude. We're almost positive we know what this is, but we've got to do some more testing to know for sure."

"Can't I come back tomorrow for them?" I asked.

"No, Dorris," Dr. Blake said gravely, shaking his head. "You don't realize how sick you are. And you may get sicker."

"What are the tests like?" I sighed with impatience.

Dr. Blake explained the different tests and what they can achieve and as he continued, the severity of the situation began to sink in. "There's a method called the electromyogram," Dr. Blake said. "EMG for short. We'd use a recording of muscle activity to stimulate one of your nerves — it feels like a quick jab, but it's safe. Anyway, then we could tell if your nerve conduction is slowed or blocked by looking at the speed of the electricity traveling along the nerve. However, it's a half-hour-long test and, since we already know signals are moving along your nerves slowly, it seems pointless."

He sighed. "I think we'd better do a spinal tap, Dorris."

All the doctors agreed that a spinal tap would be necessary in the diagnosis and, after describing the process to me, they scheduled it for the next morning.

"First of all," Dr. Jeffrey Hecht told me, "be aware that this sounds a lot worse than it is. It's more uncomfortable than it is painful, and you'll have anesthesia if you choose. You may have a headache afterwards, but nothing you can't handle after all this. Okay?"

I nodded.

"All right," Dr. Hecht went on. "What we're going to do is stick a needle into your lower back and between your vertebrae. There's a sac of this fluid called cerebrospinal fluid, which bathes the nerve roots of the spinal chord. We'll draw some of that fluid from you and then we'll look at it to see what this is you've got."

"How are you going to know from that?" I asked.

"Well, if there is a lot of protein in the fluid and there's a normal cell count, then our suspicions will be confirmed," he said. "If you have this condition, your fluid will be abnormal."

It bothered me that they were all so sure that I had this mysterious disease. "And what if I don't have it?" I asked.

"Then we try something else," he said.

Great. I'm never going to get out of here. All I could do was think about work and the commitments I'd for several hotels and federal buildings. I kept telling myself, *You don't have time to be sick, Dorris! You can't afford to be sick!*

My health was waning, but my spirit would not be suppressed by my ailing body. Yet I could not ignore that I was being strapped into a special bed that tilted and rotated me every so often so my skin wouldn't atrophy or develop bedsores. And although I looked like a hospital patient, I still didn't feel like one.

My sisters visited and my son Michael had come from college to see me, but it was far from a happy reunion. Later that evening, my dear friend, Betty Micheli, came to see me when my assistant called her to tell her I was in the hospital. Betty was my realtor when I was looking for a bed-and-breakfast to buy in 1990, and in the two years that we had been friends, I don't believe she had ever seen me downcast. Even if she had, she was in no way prepared for my complete transformation in appearance and energy level.

"Dorris was always ahead of the pack," Betty Micheli recalled. "Full of life and ambition. But when I went to see her, I wouldn't have given you a penny for her chances. I expected Dorris to die, she looked so bad. But her mind was alert. She looked up at me and said, 'This is awful, you've got to get me out of here.'"

That's all I could think about: getting out of there. Around eight o'clock that night, I realized how lucky I was to be there and not all alone at home. I truly felt "deathly ill," literally sick enough to die. I had a horrible headache and I couldn't stop vomiting. There was green foam coming out of me and I had a fever. I imagined this was what it felt like to be poisoned or have a gallstone attack. Except that this seemed worse.

I remember pulling myself along the wall to get to the bathroom, but passing out before I got there, which scared my family half to death as well as frightening the nurses. They sponged out my mouth, gave me painkillers, and advised me to rest.

All along I had been assuring everyone that I was fine and that I'd be out of the hospital in no time, but I think the seriousness of my situation was finally testing even *my* confidence. If it hadn't yet, it would the next day.

On Monday morning I was moved to Intensive Care because I was considered in critical condition. I was completely paralyzed. I couldn't move anything from my ears down, but even though my chest muscles were affected and my breathing was weak, I still didn't require an iron lung, which, I was told, made me lucky.

But I didn't feel too lucky when, lying on my side, I felt the needle for the spinal tap as it broke through my flesh and dug deep into my lower back. Dr. Hecht was right; it was not painful, it was just a little uncomfortable. Still, I was glad when it was over.

I was calm — until Dr. Blake gathered my family around my bed and announced the results of the test.

"Dorris," he said, "the results of your spinal tap confirmed my fears. You have a problem with your nerves, a condition called Guillain Barré Syndrome. Your immune system has attacked your nervous system," he went on, "and that is why your muscles are paralyzed."

My family broke into frantic interrogation, and even though Dr. Blake responded to each question as best he could, they weren't satisfied with the answers.

"The problem," Dr. Blake told us, "is that not much is known about GBS because the symptoms and recovery rates are so varied. It may affect people so little that they never even go into the hospital — they just feel strange sensations like tingling hands, feet or face, or they get easily fatigued.

"Other people, on the other hand, are paralyzed so extensively that they their faces droop and they can't move their eyes. One thing we've been worried about with you, Dorris, is that your breathing muscles will get too weak and you'll have to go on a ventilator. That's one of the most dangerous complications. It can be very disabling."

He went on to explain that Guillain Barré Syndrome is an acute peripheral neuropathology, which means that it affects the peripheral nervous system. My nerves, he said, were unable to transmit the signals from my brain efficiently because my immune system was attacking my own nerves and stripping them of their outer coating, called myelin sheaths. The myelin sheath, and possibly the covered conducting part of the nerve, called the axon, were damaged from the attack and the signals between them and the brain are impaired.

As a result, my muscles had lost their ability to respond to my brain's commands. Not only that, but my brain was also receiving fewer sensory signals from the rest of my body, making it hard for me to feel textures, heat, pain, and other sensations. The signals that my brain was receiving, however, were mostly the wrong signals, causing the sensations of numbness, pain, tingling, vibration and crawling under the skin in my feet, my hands, gums, and face.

"All kinds of nerves are affected by GBS — the nerves that tell us to move, feel, breathe, swallow, talk and smile," Dr. Blake informed us. "It's usually when the motor system starts failing that people first go to the doctor. They'll notice that their muscles are weak, aching and cramping. They can't easily lift things and their leg and hip muscles stop working, so it's difficult to walk or even stand. That's generally when people realize they need help. Or when their facial muscles collapse and their smiles are lopsided. But the real danger is in the effects on the automatic nerves involved in regulating blood pressure, heart rate, body temperature, vision and kidney function."

As I listened to him tell us about this strange disease, I heard what he was saying, but I couldn't imagine that I had something like what he was explaining. It reminded me of the poor, unfortunate bride struck by polio on her wedding day. I knew I couldn't relate to her and I knew I wasn't going to ever have to. When I heard him say that I'd probably be sick for a long time, I summoned up what little energy I had to shake my head and say, "No, I can't have a disease like that."

"Well, Dorris," Dr. Blake said, "I'm sorry, but it looks like you do. GBS is hard to diagnose — mostly because of its high variety of symptoms — and, in its early stages, it's easily mistaken for pneumonia, the flu or the common cold. Many people are sent home to rest, only to get worse and worse and then to find out they have Guillain Barré Syndrome. Other times it's easy to predict that it's GBS just by listening to a patient's symptoms, but there are so many tests that must be done to be certain, that it takes forever to actually make the diagnosis.

"Like with you, we were suspicious that this is what we were dealing with, but we had to make sure. But you were luckier than some; I've heard of it taking six spinal taps before the doctors could be positive it was GBS."

Making it even harder to diagnose, Dr. Blake told us, is the fact that the symptoms can develop in a matter of hours or in a matter of weeks. So, doctors rarely predict that the patient has GBS when the symptoms first occur.

"In fact," Dr. Blake explained, "because objective evidence is hard to find in the earliest stages, patients sometimes have a hard time convincing doctors that there's anything physically wrong at all. When the common symptom of heightened sensitivity or another strange feeling is present, it's even been written off as some kind of emotional disturbance."

I thought about that. I couldn't imagine a doctor not believing that a patient's symptoms were real and I questioned whether Dr. Blake might be exaggerating.

However, I later learned that quite often this is actually the case. One woman I talked to told me that, no matter what she did, the hospital staff refused to support her.

"They thought I was playing it up," she said. "The doctor told me just to go home, and I said, 'No, I can't go home. I am too weak.'

"They looked at me with these patient looks on their faces and I said, 'Here, watch me walk.' I slid myself to the floor and collapsed onto the floor after I'd taken one step. They believed me then."

"There are some distinguishing symptoms," Dr. Blake told me and my family. "In GBS the weakness and the abnormal sensations are the same on both sides of the body. It also tends to move from the extremities in toward the torso. It typically starts in the feet, moves up to the knees and then to the hips. From there it can go to the chest and then the face. This is because the arms and legs are the farthest away from the brain and the signals between them are the most susceptible to interruption along the way."

Dr. Blake said that it's usually a general feeling of weakness, numbness, and cramping that precedes the paralysis, which can be preceded by a general feeling of weakness, pins and needles and even slight cramping. He said that the progression of the weakness usually occurs in the following order: toe and foot muscles, then to hamstrings and glutei, then to anterior and adductor muscles of the thigh, then to finger and hand muscles, then arm muscles, then shoulder muscles, then trunk muscles, then respiratory muscles, tongue, pharynx and esophagus. As it advances, the paralysis generalizes, but becomes more severe in the extremities.

"Its tendency to move upward through the body is why we want to keep testing you and monitor you carefully for a while," Dr. Blake said. "We want to make sure it doesn't travel any farther up than it already has. I promise to tell you everything else I know tomorrow, but right now it is crucial that we do some more tests to see how far the paralysis has spread."

The doctor told my family that they could see me only five minutes every hour because I had to be under constant supervision. As they left, my sister asked me what I wanted to do about the business, which, at the time, I thought odd.

Yes, some of my clients needed to be contacted, but the business? Why was it in question? I was convinced that I would pick up where I left off on Thursday, and that would be that. "Let's wait before making a decision," I said, a little hurt that she didn't hold the faith that I did.

For the rest of the day and on into Tuesday, the nurses and the doctors stood around me and watched the paralysis advance. It was attacking other parts of my body and they were worried it would get into my lungs or eyes. I asked them why they weren't doing anything to stop the paralysis from spreading.

"There's nothing that can be done at this point," one of the doctors said.

"Then how can I get better?" I demanded. "I don't have forever."

Even though the room was packed with doctors, all of them fully able to hear me, no one answered. I knew they couldn't tell me what they didn't know themselves, but I also knew had to be something that could be done.

"Be patient," Dr. Hecht said with finality. "We're doing everything we can, Dorris."

"How long will I be sick?" I asked, my impatience becoming evident.

"It lasts different lengths of time for different people," Dr. Hecht said. "For some, it is permanently disabling. For others, it just passes away with time. That's what we're trying to determine now, Dorris. We're watching you to see how far it has progressed and how much you can expect to recover. But we have to do a lot of tests on you for the next few days before we can give you a fair prognosis."

Well, he hadn't given me an answer, but I still knew I wouldn't be sick for long. That wasn't an option for me, and I never even considered it. I knew God would heal me. My life might not go back to normal — I might never wear high heels again — but I had faith that God wouldn't let me down. I knew that, as long as I was willing to help myself, I could rely on Him. He would answer me if no one else could.

"Was there anything I could have done to prevent it?" I asked after a while.

"Probably not," he said. "It's really unpredictable, and even though only one in 100,000 people get it, virtually anyone can. It doesn't matter if you're young or old, male or female, a runner or a couch potato. It does tend to attack people over forty more often than younger people, but it is actually more common in the young and in the old of a population."

In a study that I read soon after, I learned that GBS is extremely rare in children less than two years old but that, of the thirty percent of GBS patients who are less than twenty years old, two-thirds are younger than eight. That same study said that GBS occurs in three males per every two women and that Caucasians are more likely to be attacked by GBS than non-Caucasians.

"So anyone can get it," Dr. Blake said. "It's not contagious, so you couldn't have avoided it, and it's not inherited, so you couldn't have predicted it. In fact, the exact cause of Guillain Barré Syndrome is not known. A syndrome actually means a group of symptoms that collectively characterize an abnormality. So GBS is really one big symptom that is triggered by something else that has already happened in the body. The thing is, there are a lot of possible triggers including insect stings, surgery, pregnancy, stress, trauma, alcohol abuse and viral, respiratory and gastrointestinal infections."

"A lot of cases begin after a viral infection," Dr. Hecht said. "Anytime between a few days and a few weeks afterward. Some viral infections are more frequently associated with Guillain Barré, like infectious mononucleosis, viral hepatitis, HIV, cytomegalovirus (CMV), hepatitis, rabies, and herpes simplex infection."

Dr. Hecht went on to say that scientists were investigating certain characteristics of these viruses to see if they activate the immune system in any way, perhaps making it less critical about what cells it recognizes as its own. "If this were the case," he added, "immune cells might be allowed to attack the myelin. It is also possible that the virus changes the cells in the nervous system so that the immune system treats them as foreign cells."

"But viral infections are just one of the many triggers of GBS," Dr. Blake reminded me. "It has also occurred with porphyria, campylobacter jejuni and lymphoma, and, quite often it is preceded by an injection, an immunization like the flu shot. In the winters of 1976 and 1977, there was a Guillain Barré Syndrome epidemic in patients who had the swine flu vaccination. Basically, anything that triggers an auto-immune reaction could potentially generate the syndrome. In other words, the immune system has had a little run, and it's taking it a while to wind down."

"Looking for something to do," Dr. Hecht nodded.

"But," Dr. Blake said, "you couldn't have done anything to stop it, that's for sure. You might not have helped it too much. Since you're such a fighter, I assume you didn't make it very easy for the attack to run its course, which it needed to do. I don't know this for sure, but you might not have been hit so hard if you hadn't fought it so much."

Well, I thought, *I'm going to keep fighting it, too!* I never questioned that I would be one of the GBS victims to make a full, speedy recovery. I didn't see any other way for me to be. I was too anxious to get out of there and get on with my life.

Eventually, after four days of testing and watching me day in and day out, the doctors reached a conclusion. They stopped the testing and moved me into another room. In the meantime, they had apparently called my entire family to come to the hospital and talk with them because my sisters, brothers, and sons were all there. All my siblings still lived in Tennessee, but my older son Arthur had come all the way from Charleston.

It was my understanding that they were there to hear the prognosis with me, though I later found out that whoever had called Arthur told him that I was dying, and that he should come to the hospital right away. So much for hope and "anything is possible." The doctors seemed to have written me off already. I'm just glad I didn't know what they were saying at the time.

"Dorris," the neurosurgeon said, "after all those tests, we've finally got some information for you. Just hang in there a minute longer, while I go talk to your sons real quick. Then we'll come fill you in. Okay?"

I found that strange and I wondered what was so secretive about my condition that she couldn't tell me first.

"No," I said, as she was walking out the door. "That's not okay. It's me who's sick. I'm the one you should be talking to. I want to know when I can get out of here."

"Honey," she said, "you can't move."

"Well I know that," I said. "The question is, when will I be able to move?"

"We're going to talk about that in just a second," she said. "I'll be right back with your family."

Not five minutes had passed before I heard my brothers sniffling and my sisters crying right outside my door. They were discussing my death.

It's an indescribable, wrenching feeling to hear your family crying over your death when you're certain you're not dying. I couldn't control my anger at their lack of faith. Although they always loved me, they never quite understood my determination. I had always maintained a cheerful, jolly outlook on life and the fact that they were so blindly listening to a doctor's dark description amazed and hurt me. I couldn't believe how quick the doctors were to predict the fate of someone they hardly knew at all, based solely on medical knowledge. And then to lay out for my family such a horrible image of my future without being positive of its truth!

Of course, I knew my neurosurgeon was wrong, but my family had no way of knowing that. Their ignorance of GBS kept them from knowing what to think. To them, the doctors were the authorities, and their prediction was my fate. For me, however, my faith is my fate.

"Stop it now," I said to my family when the doctor opened the door and led them inside. "I'm not going to die. I'm too alive to die."

The looks on their faces told me they believed the doctors over me. They were discouraged, and they'd made up their minds, but that only increased my strength and determination. I looked over at the neurosurgeon and waited for her to give her ruling.

Exactly one week after my flight from South Carolina and my first signs of fatigue and muscle aches, I learned just how badly those aches and pains had affected me: I would never walk again.

Arthur made a choking sound, signifying he was about to cry. I looked at him sharply. "I most certainly will walk again," I said, looking at each of my family members individually. "You know I'm not a sitter! I'm a doer!"

"You may never be able to take care of yourself," one of my brothers said.

"You guys need to lighten up," I said, glancing at each one of their faces. "I'll be out of here in no time."

"You'll have to stay here for a while," the doctor said, clearing her throat. "You'll be sick for a long time, Dorris."

I was a businesswoman, which prevented me from depending on other people or wasting time in a hospital. I had too much to do, and there was no way I would allow myself to lie around in bed all day "for a long time." I knew there was some way I could speed this thing up. And I knew I'd find out what to do.

It was finally time to break a new record; take on something even bigger than the biggest project I'd done for the U.S. Navy. I had just signed the contract with myself to restore health to my own body.

Chapter Three:

Led By Faith

"Would you tell me please, which way I ought to go from here?"
"That depends a good deal on where you want to get to."
– Lewis Carroll, *Alice in Wonderland*

"I'M SORRY, HONEY," I said, "but we've got to do a whole lot better than that! I don't have that kind of time to be wasting in bed. I've got a business to run!"

The neurosurgeon stared at me, blinked and said, "I'm sorry, too, Dorris, but this is something that you've got to deal with. Guillain Barré Syndrome is a very serious neurological disorder and you've been hit pretty hard. Your chances of regaining normal functions, such as walking and breathing independently, are . . . slim, at best."

"You don't know me. I will get better," I assured the doctor.

"All right, Dorris. If that's the way you want to feel, okay."

"Yes," I said, "that's how I want to feel: better. And I have no doubt at all that that's exactly how I'm going to feel. But you're the doctor and I need your help."

The neurosurgeon furrowed her eyebrows and regarded me suspiciously. I knew she was trying to determine if I was kidding or if I was in denial about the prognosis she'd just made.

"Actually," I continued, "I need help from all the doctors. Now, I'm paralyzed at the moment, so could you go round up all the doctors that know anything about my case for me? I have questions for all of them. I want to understand everything thoroughly."

The doctor left without a word, having decided that I was neither kidding nor in denial, but rather that I was a "problem patient." And maybe I was, but the way I looked at it, problems always require a lot more attention than peace.

"Now," I said to the neurosurgeon when she returned and to the five doctors who followed her, "I understand that I'm going to be sick for a few months or maybe more. I need to know if there are any ways I can recover sooner than that. I need to know everything I can do to hurry this along."

"You're lucky not to be on a respirator already," the neurosurgeon commented curtly.

"I'd like to know if there is any way I can speed up my recovery, and I'd like to know how it can be done," I repeated, addressing the other doctors attentively huddled around my bed.

They seemed to be sincerely considering my request, at least until their attention was redirected toward the neurosurgeon as she opened the door, called in a nurse, and told her that I needed an injection of something that sounded like a sedative.

"No, ma'am," I said. "This disease has already got me sluggish enough. All I want is some answers so I can understand my condition."

"All we know is that you'll be here a while and that it is unlikely that you'll be walking out when you leave. So look around the room and take everything in because this will be your view for a long time. This is your new home."

"Not me — I won't be here very long at all," I said.

And I had my mind set that I wouldn't be. My life had been turned upside down, but I had survived so far. I lay there feeling like one of those hotel rooms after we'd gutted it, anxious to begin the rebuilding process and ready to launch myself completely into the job. Accustomed to managing large crews and having them carry out my orders, I felt confident that I could manage my recovery. Since my approach had always proved successful in the design contracting business, I responded to this crew of professionals in the same way I handled my work teams: "Let's get going!"

My lifelong tendency to be demanding worked in my favor when the doctors at the hospital reacted in a positive manner to my determination. They told me that they'd never had a GBS patient with the energy I had.

"This place will never be the same," one of the doctors told me. "Never before has a patient interviewed the doctors."

But I couldn't imagine it being any other way. After all, this was my life we were talking about here, and there's nothing more important to a person than his own life. Since then, I have heard many people stricken with GBS say that a thorough inquisition of their doctors about the condition was significantly helpful in improving their attitudes and outlooks. Not only do patients who do a little interrogation become encouraged that everything possible is being done, but they also feel more in control.

"Even though I couldn't lift my head from my pillow or even move the right side of my face," a patient in the rehabilitation stage of GBS told me later, "I asked my doctors a ton of questions. You've got to know everything there is to know about what's happening to your body and what you can expect to happen next — so find out! Doctors are responsible for answering your questions."

However, voluntary encouragement and reassurance are generally lacking in the initial care of GBS. In fact, there is a tendency among doctors to be overly pessimistic. One man I talked to was told that the odds were against his wife's survival.

"She hadn't talked and she'd had her eyes closed for a month when they told me not to be too hopeful," he remembered. "I'm just glad she didn't hear their prognosis — I don't think she would have made it." His wife, however, did not hear the doctors' discouraging words and she has since achieved seventy-five percent recovery.

Doctors are not trying to transmit negativity or hopelessness in their interactions with patients and their families. Patients vary a lot in recovery and, when faced with new GBS patients exhibiting similar symptoms, the doctor is prone to make a prognosis based on a previous patient's outcome. Indeed, it is easy to underestimate an individual's strength or capacity to recover.

"I kept telling the doctors that I would be better before they knew it," a GBS patient in the rehabilitation stage said. "But no one believed me. Up until then, I hadn't questioned anything my doctors were doing for me. But when they treated my faith in God's healing ability like a child's silly fantasy, I decided that I needed more help than what they were willing to give me. I found out about a local specialist in neurological disorders and he provided me with the care that I needed in order to get better."

Making sure that you're getting everything possible out of your caretakers is very important. Do not hesitate to ask for further assistance or to demand clarification.

One woman I spoke with said that when her doctor told her that she'd never walk again, she fell into a deep depression. "It hadn't even dawned on me that this was going to be permanent," she said. "I'd been thinking I'd be out of there within a week, and now they were telling me I was handicapped! About two weeks after they'd made that prognosis, I realized I needed to cheer up and focus on recovering. I asked one of the nurses and she told me about a hospital support group for people with spinal cord injuries. No one had even mentioned this to me, and it was something that I needed. It gave me an outlet for all the feelings that I'd been dealing with so I could concentrate on what really mattered: getting better."

Most patients would benefit — both emotionally and physically — from informative counseling with a person knowledgeable in GBS. Although doctors safeguard against fostering false hope in their patients and are understandably hesitant to reveal more than what they can be sure of, simply providing some statistical information about recovery from GBS would greatly benefit most patients' attitudes.

With my viewpoint that you can never find out enough, I decided to do my own research on GBS. I asked the hospital social worker to bring me any literature she could find about the disorder. "I need to know everything that I can find out," I told her.

She brought me all sorts of books, journals, magazines and photocopies of articles. Unfortunately, most of the material dealt with the unknown aspects of GBS. There is much more information today — especially through the Internet — than there was then, but it's important to know that anyone can get this disease and the public should be aware of it and its symptomatic similarities to the flu.

Still, there was enough information available for me to learn a great deal. Throughout my research I have found that, unlike many doctors' outlook on recovery, statistical evidence is relatively optimistic and shows that most patients' chances for recovery are good. Even the most severe GBS cases are likely to recover to some extent. Fifty to ninety percent of all GBS patients recover completely or are left only mild to moderate residual effects that don't significantly interfere with their everyday functions. Many recovered patients, for example, often feel weak.

Although I'm sure it's not nearly as common as muscle weakness and numbness, I have heard that some patients notice the shedding of the skin on their hands and feet. The numb, prickly sensation that often occurs in the feet and legs is much more typical. "Foot drop," a painful, tingling sensation like paralysis in that it makes it impossible to move the foot, is commonly a long-term effect for GBS patients. It is hard to walk without tripping. There are, however, devices that assist people with foot drop to walk.

Although some patients do occasionally suffer from debilitating symptoms after they have reached their full recovery potential, most of the aftereffects are more frustrating than disabling.

The achy muscles, for example, might make certain activities difficult from time to time, but they are rarely so severe that all social or work activity must cease.

Despite doctors' bleak, gloomy prognoses, only five to fifteen percent of Guillain Barré patients are left with severe, long-term disabilities that actually prevent them from leading normal lifestyles. Less than five percent die, and the majority of deaths associated with Guillain Barré Syndrome result from heart or lung complications. Only about three percent are attacked by GBS a second time.

To the doctors' credit, prognosis cannot fairly be predicted. Few things about GBS are constant, and recovery is not one of them. Doctors usually guess at the speed and extent of a patient's recovery, basing their estimate on the patient's age and general health, the time it took for the patient to be diagnosed, the amount of damage done to the nerves and the caliber of the patient's response to the treatment.

Because doctors have no way of making certain that their prognoses are accurate, patients would benefit greatly from some kind of comprehensive overview of the recovery statistics from GBS to garner hope and determination to get well quickly.

The patient deserves to understand and be informed about everything concerning the condition. It is especially important to know what is going on inside the body — why he can't move his legs, has lost control of his bowels, has strange sensations in his arms and so forth — in addition to being privy to what is going on around him. Special attention should be given to patients who are unable to communicate because they're on a ventilator. Because they can't ask questions or express concerns, it's easy for these patients to get scared.

"I remember feeling like I was locked into this little world that no one else really knew about," one patient said. "To top it off, I could only see out of my peripheral vision, so I couldn't tell what was going on a lot of the time.

"I guess one of the nurses could tell I was frightened because one day she came in with an Etch-a-Sketch for me to use to write questions. I was happy to have it, but my hands were so numb that I couldn't write legibly. The next day the same nurse brought in a chart that she had made. She had picked out a few finger gestures and given them meanings like yes and no, 'I need to go to the bathroom,' 'I hurt' and so forth. She put the chart on the wall across from my bed, and I never panicked again. Just knowing how to get something across to my doctors helped me tremendously."

To have tubes going in and coming out of your body and machines beeping every time you breathe can be distressing and confusing. Anything that can relieve these responses and ease the anxiety is undeniably helpful.

It is, for example, important that someone talk to the patients' families, even if the patient himself is not unduly distressed about the condition. The reactions and attitudes of family members can have a significant effect on the patient and cause him to wonder what mixed messages he's receiving. Doctors should, in other words, go to great lengths to assure that the patient is not left in the dark about any aspect of his condition.

One man left alone much of the time while he was in the hospital with GBS, remembers being terrified. "I was constantly in a state of panic," he said. "No one explained to me that the strange sensations I felt in my legs and shoulders and hands were normal! I thought I was going crazy whenever I woke up and couldn't tell where my hands were without actually looking at them. If only a nurse or someone had said, 'This is what you can expect to feel.'"

Doctors can rarely take the time to inform GBS patients fully about their situation and what can possibly be done. Hence, patients or family members need to ask questions. More often than not, however, it is the patient who is the expert and not the doctor. In fact, I met a man who had actually been interviewed by his doctors!

"At first they made me wear a mask because they thought I had something contagious. When they figured out that it was GBS, they got all excited and they asked me all sorts of questions and took notes the whole time," the fully-recovered patient told me. "They had these books that they would look at and then look up at me and say, 'Now, it says here that the paralysis usually starts in the feet. Is that what happened with you?'"

Another patient, still in the primary stage of GBS, did not observe such a blatant ignorance among his doctors, but the unfamiliarity with the disease, she told me, was still apparent. "I was really discouraged," she said. "I couldn't blink my eyes for three days and no one could give me a clear prognosis or even a suggestion. I kept asking questions and the more I asked, the more I realized that that no one knew much of anything about GBS."

Unfortunately, this is often the case and it can be very disheartening. If the doctors can't give you the information you need, have someone do the research for you. Just knowing about the disease is usually enough to provide at least a little encouragement for most patients.

"If I hadn't done the research I did," the patient whose questions were unanswered told me, "I would have lost hope the day they made the diagnosis."

Both from the research I did and my overall experience, I learned that once the condition is understood, it becomes easier to accept it and move on. I realized that there was a good chance that I'd recover, which really pushed me to do everything possible to get better. Although some people find it even more discouraging to hear that it may be a while before they are well again, most are just happy to find out that they *will* be well again.

For me, the prognosis of how long it would take was more of an incentive than a deterrent to push my doctors and myself. I had faith that I could do better than what these doctors were predicting, and I knew I had the means to prove it.

"Most people can't see the light in the tunnel for a long time after they're first diagnosed with Guillain Barré Syndrome," said Dr. Blake later. "It's tough to look the lion in the mouth. Most people aren't able to keep that positive spirit going. Dorris is the exception to the rule. I've never had anyone with that type of illness who was as positive as she was."

Despite the fact that I was not a well-behaved patient — pestering the doctors to explain things to me and to help me recover quickly — I think they liked my outlook. So much of my life had been about doing business and helping others professionally. Now I needed help, and the idea of not being in control made me nervous. I kept asking what I could do to help myself and they would advise me to be patient. But I didn't have time to be patient. After all, I had to get back to work as soon as possible!

I stayed in Intensive Care for seventeen days and I was in critical condition for six of those. Although I was receiving pain medication every four hours, I was still mentally alert, and I was constantly asking the doctors why they were going to do things, and what was the purpose and the expected benefit. I wanted to know everything there was to know, and, to their credit, they usually offered thorough explanations. The most important thing I ever asked them was "What is there that we're not doing now?"

They explained to me that there are therapies that lessen the severity of the illness and accelerate the recovery, but that treatment is based on trial and error, and the methods are highly individualized. There was no concrete definition for what would work best for me. Besides that, they said, the benefits of some of the treatments are questionable. The treatment could take many months and some patients continue to get worse, while others react quite well.

They told me about high-dose immunoglobulin therapy, in which doctors inject the same proteins that the immune system uses naturally to attack invading organisms. Another treatment they told me about was steroid hormones called corticosteroids, which, they said, were rarely effective and could even be harmful.

My fever being so high, however, there was really only one choice they had at this point: plasmapheresis. Through this procedure, the doctors told me, the antibodies and other toxic substances in my blood could be removed.

The first step is to extract the blood from the body. Once that is done, the blood is processed so that the red and white blood cells can be separated from the plasma. After separation, the blood cells are returned to the body without the plasma and the body quickly replaces the plasma.

"It's an effective treatment for people like you," Dr. Hecht said. "It works best when implemented at an early stage of the disorder. It's a dangerous procedure, but if the risks were greater than your current risks, then I wouldn't suggest it at all. Its potential complications are why it's reserved for patients with severe weakness and who are expected to benefit greatly from it. And I think you could definitely benefit from it. If you agree to it, we can start the blood treatment tomorrow."

"How risky is it?" I asked, even though I'd already made up my mind that I would start the treatment as soon as possible.

"Well, I think the figure is three deaths for every 10,000 procedures," Dr. Hecht said. "Every year there are somewhere between 20,000 to 30,000 plasmapheresis blood treatments performed in the United States. Between 1978 and 1983, plasmapheresis has been associated with a total of fifty deaths worldwide. Sixteen of those deaths were caused by complications with the cardiac system, and fourteen were complications of the respiratory system. Some of the other twenty deaths were results of hepatitis, an allergic reaction called anaphylaxis, and an infection called sepsis."

The rest of the causes of death during plasmapheresis are quite complicated, and it wasn't until later that I understood what they all meant. They include pulmonary thromboembolism, an obstruction of a blood vessel in the lungs; vascular perforation, the breaking of an ulcer through the blood vessels; and a systemic hemorrhage with disseminated intravascular coagulation, which is basically just internal bleeding caused by shock, inducing blood clotting throughout the body.

That day, however, I was hardly listening to all the complications affecting other patients. I was going to be just fine, I was sure of it. I waited patiently for Dr. Hecht to finish explaining the various risk factors and then said, "Let's do it! I don't have time to be lying in this bed all day doing nothing."

I signed a consent form by scratching an X, since I couldn't write. Then, of course, I started asking questions. First of all, I wanted to know how this procedure was going to help me.

"No one knows for sure why it works," the Doctor Hecht. "Maybe because there are harmful parts of the immune system in the plasma. Another idea is that the chemical messengers that the lymph cells send with the circulating reactants, so common after infectious illnesses, are contributors to the illnesses' progress. So, when they are removed, the disease slows down. We're not sure. But it does keep the symptoms from getting worse, and it does speed up recovery. It's a really short-lived effect, which is fine in an acute syndrome like Guillain Barré. It just means that we might have to repeat the treatment three to five times over the next two weeks."

I asked what they were going to do during the procedure and how I was going to feel, and the doctors explained the process to me, noting that there would be a lot of nurses present during the procedure.

They promised the incision would be in a place not usually exposed, and that the scar would go away with time. I would not be unconscious during the treatment, but I would be sedated, and I could expect to feel pretty woozy.

"Okay, now tell me all the wonderful things I'll be getting out of all this suffering," I said.

"Well, you're lucky, Dorris," Dr. Hecht said, "because the patients who have severe GBS and who begin plasmapheresis within two weeks of the onset of their symptoms are the ones who benefit the most out of this procedure. You won't be noticing any immediate effects. In fact, you might get worse at first. But the overall time it takes your body regain its strength will be shortened — you'll get out of here sooner! Also, if you should have to go on a ventilator at any point, the plasmapheresis will keep you from being on it very long."

The next day I was glad they'd told me the benefits of plasmapheresis because if I hadn't known that it was going to help, it might have been unbearable. It was excruciating, almost causing me to jump when they cut the hole in my neck and slid the tube into my jugular vein.

"I —"

"Hush! Be still, Dorris," the doctor told me over and over again.

So I couldn't talk and I couldn't move the whole time they were sucking my blood from my neck. I felt like a slimy fish. It was awful.

The doctors left an opening in my neck so that they wouldn't have to cut it more than once. The treatment is usually repeated five or six times and can only be performed every two days. After the two-hour process, you're left completely lifeless. I went through the blood treatment every two days for ten days, dreading it every time.

I felt my worst during my fourth treatment. I wasn't in as much pain as I'd been in during the previous procedures, but I remember feeling empty, like everything inside had stopped working. There was a whirlwind of activity around me and the sounds of the doctors' voices were all swirled together. One doctor's voice, however, stood out.

"She's awful weak," I heard him say. "I'm not sure she's going to be able to stand it."

It seemed like there were more people bustling around me than there had been before and all doing something different.

The confusion of the movement made me feel nauseous, so I closed my eyes. I remember hearing something come to me like the wind. Then, in a far-off voice, someone said, "We've lost her. We aren't getting any pulse."

I opened my eyes. I was looking down at the tops of the doctors' heads and at my own body! Everything was illuminated with a bluish hue, and I couldn't hear anything. Everyone but me seemed to be moving quickly — pulling the tubes out of me and giving me shots and electrical shocks — frantic and concerned. But I was more calm and more content than I'd ever felt before. It felt the way I'd always imagined it would feel to float on a cloud.

Suddenly, out of the silence, I heard a whispering sound. Then, with a soft and comforting breeze, Jesus came toward me in a bright cloud. There were wispy white angels all around Him, welcoming me. It was such a beautiful sight, and my eyes filled with tears at the power of the moment. And then, in a smooth, tranquil gesture, Jesus reached His hands toward me.

I felt a firm, soothing hand on my own and just as I did, I heard a doctor shout, "I believe we've got a pulse!"

Instantly, I was back on the bed. I'd had no sense that I was falling or that I was moving, but there I was, lying on the table and surrounded by motion. I looked up at space where the clouds had just been. All I could see were the fluorescent lights. But I knew He was still there, smiling down at me.

Chapter Four:
Breaking All the Rules

W HEN JESUS REACHED OUT to me, He didn't physically touch me. He reached into my soul and touched my life in a much more powerful way. For some reason, He had granted me a second chance at life. Maybe He'd wanted me to live so I could go on to help people, or perhaps He was simply showing His appreciation for my faith. I know that if I hadn't already had faith, and if I hadn't been willing to fight for my life, He wouldn't have come to save me.

Why He had blessed me, however, doesn't matter. The results of His visit do: my faith in Him and my dedication to Him were reinforced and expanded. He was more real to me than He'd ever been, and I knew then that I would never be the same. He had saved my life in many more ways than one and I wanted nothing more than to show my thanks.

As a quiet young nurse covered me with two blankets and pushed me back to my room, I vowed to show God how grateful I was, and still am, for His love.

I'm going to do everything I can to devote myself to Him, I remember thinking as the nurses helped me into bed. *And, as soon as I*

53

can, I'll serve Him by sharing His love with others in need of help.

That thought — that I had to get better not only for my sake and for God's sake, but also for the sake of other sick people — that was my incentive. I kept that in my mind at all times, and it became my anchoring motivation any time things got rough. And, boy, did things get rough!

"Dorris had a tough first two or three weeks," Dr. Blake said later. "She didn't get dramatically better after the plasmapheresis, but it stabilized things, enough to where we thought her illness was turning around."

Apparently, this is most often the case: the disease tends to get worse before it gets better. The symptoms generally increase in severity over the first two weeks and, by the third week, nearly ninety percent of the patients are at their weakest.

By the sixth week, however, all GBS patients have hit their worst degree of weakness. The downhill stage of Guillain Barré can last anywhere from a few days to a few weeks, and it is at this point that most people are confined to a hospital bed and watched carefully for complications.

Dr. Blake told me that after this period of worsening, most patients hit a plateau for a while — again, anywhere from a few days to a few weeks. During this stage, paralysis and weakness neither improve nor decline, and it is easy for patients to get discouraged at their inability to recover rapidly.

Improvement, however, will come. And that's what I kept telling myself.

I'd learned that, in direct opposition to the onset of GBS, its retreat moves down the body, so that the upper parts of the body recover first and the legs and feet regain feeling last. Even when I was still in the downhill stage I thought every once in a while that I could feel my shoulder a little bit. I would get so excited and then I'd come to realize that it was just my imagination.

I couldn't wait to be able to feel and move again, and I sought out everything I could find about my future recovery. Most of what I found said that once a patient begins to improve, specific progress typically comes on a daily basis. The stronger the patient gets, however, the harder it is for him to note any improvement, since progress slows down once endurance is built.

I read one article that said that, in order to keep their spirits up, patients should appreciate their progress on a weekly level at first and on a monthly level as the recovery progresses. I especially liked that article because it seemed to be aware of the patient's true well-being.

Most of the literature I'd found was very medical and scientific, giving Guillain Barré a cold, impersonal and distant tone. Instead of focusing on the complicated statistical data like most everything else I'd read, this article focused on the fact that the reader is going to recover and that it's going to be a satisfying process, helping me handle my fear.

Another article that I read when I was already out of rehab I remember clearly. It was about the swimmer Rowdy Gaines, who won three gold medals in the 1984 Los Angeles Olympics before he was hit with GBS. The inspirational story, which I found in the July 15, 1995, issue of *People,* follows Gaines through the onset of GBS and on into recovery. It wasn't his story that was particularly memorable, though; it was his attitude.

"The day I got out of the hospital they had to carry me up the steps to the pool," said Gaines.

I remember reading that, and thinking, *now there's a motivated man.* The fact that he marveled at having to be carried out of the pool and not that he went swimming the day he got out of the hospital, struck me as being self-assured and faith-filled. Gaines' determination further impressed me when I read on and learned that, even though he was not fully recovered, he'd set six world records three short years after his bout of GBS.

Still, it was the plans that Gaines was making in 1995 that impressed me the most. Although he'd qualified for the U.S. team trials in two events, he chose instead to serve as a swimming commentator on NBC. Rowdy Gaines had realized what it takes most people who've suffered a serious illness a lifetime to understand: the focus should be on future potential and not on recovering every facet of your previous lifestyle.

So many of us think that we're not better until we've completely restored our lives to the way they were before the illness struck. Gaines, however, saw his altered perspective as a refreshing opportunity.

"That's going to be so exciting," he said. "I'll have the best seat in the house."

The attitude that we have when we face our challenges is, by far, the most important factor in determining our success. In fact, had it not been for my faithful attitude and determination, I am not sure that I would have made it through the plasmapheresis, much less through recovery. But I had faith, motivation, and a positive outlook, which would help me recover quickly, if it was feasible.

The rate of recovery for GBS patients is estimated differently in different sources, but, from what I gathered, patients could recover in anywhere from six months to over two years. I was determined to be closer to the six month end.

A good indication of the extent of recovery is how soon it first begins. In other words, the shorter your plateau stage of Guillain Barré, the better. Likewise, it is generally the case that the shorter the plateau stage, the fewer the chances of long-term disability.

There is no way around the fact that Guillain Barré Syndrome has a slow-paced recovery rate. I was beginning to realize the importance of patience, but I still wanted to do anything I possibly could to speed up the pace. As I read the literature about GBS, I kept my eyes peeled for anything that was noted as beneficial. I was disappointed, however, when all I could find were reports of the significance of the medical staff's method of leading patients to recovery. Indeed, scientific and medical knowledge is crucial, but the attitudes caregivers take are much more influential. A patient could have state-of-the-art medical treatment for years upon years, but if the doctors are pessimistic and discouraging, that might not lend the necessary motivation to get better.

What I was looking for in my research, however, was something I could do to help myself. Besides, I already knew of at least three things that were more important than anything the medical staff could do for a patient: keeping a positive attitude, demanding the best from oneself and of everyone involved, and maximizing one's future. I eventually came to the conclusion that the literature that had been written was slim pickings, and that I knew better in my heart what I needed to improve quickly: faith. And I had it! Any time I looked down the road of recovery and got tired just looking at its length, I reminded myself that Jesus had come to me for a reason and that my recovery was going to be an adventure, not a chore.

"There were very few days when I recall Dorris being down, defeated, or feeling sorry for herself," Dr. Blake remembered. "That just wasn't her. From the start to the end it was always, 'I'm going to get better.'"

"She always had an upbeat attitude even though she looked awful," Betty Micheli said. "But I knew she was going to be fine when, just a few days after she'd been hospitalized, she wanted her decorating books."

I was still in Intensive Care when I started getting a little more energy. I knew I couldn't keep wasting time if I wanted to keep my business above water. I had my designers and other employees come in every day to get their orders. I had to make sure that what needed to be done was getting done so that I could collect all the money that was out floating around from the various jobs we were working on.

"She couldn't even lift a finger and she was calling me to bring her designing supplies," Betty recalled.

Dr. Blake came in every day to check on me and he constantly asked me if what I was doing was necessary. I told him I wanted to carry out what little work I could and I was going to do it. He would caution me about overextending myself.

"I don't agree with what you're doing, Dorris," he would say. "I'm worried that you'll hurt yourself."

But I knew I'd hurt myself even more if I didn't even try to get any work done. I hated for them to tell me what I could and couldn't do. They tried to tell me this was my new home, and then they made up all these rules for me. They even tried to make me eat the hospital food, but I asked my sisters to bring me food from a restaurant. I figured that since it was where I was living and since I was paying to stay there, I could do whatever I wanted.

"She would stay within the rules as long as she could make them," Betty recalled with a laugh.

I had been in Intensive Care for about seven days when some people from the March of Dimes came to see me; for what, I couldn't imagine, but I found out soon enough.

"Dorris," the head woman said, "we would like your company to design the backdrop for the March of Dimes annual fundraiser."

I didn't have to think much about it before I agreed to it. "I'll do it," I told them, "but only if I can do it my way." I already had an idea: I wanted the theme to be the light at the end of tunnel.

I was telling the March of Dimes representatives about my idea when one of the nurses called three of my doctors, who came rushing into the room.

"They're not allowed in here," one of the doctors shouted. "They're not kin to her."

"Just a minute," I said. "I'm having a little business meeting."

The doctors hated that I was doing the March of Dimes booth, but even though they tried to talk me out of a lot of things, I'd never paid them any attention. Sometimes I wonder why they even tried. I think they were ready to shoot me, but they should have known I wasn't going to let them stop me. After all, I hadn't let my illness stop me!

After seventeen days, I finally pleaded my way out of Intensive Care and onto the fifth floor of the hospital. I was still considered to be in critical condition due to the paralysis, and the doctors said that I could move into another room under one stipulation: someone had to be there with me all the time. So I asked my sisters to stay with me.

"Okay," Naomi said. "I'll do it for the first week."

For two and a half months either Margaret or Naomi or Mable Bell would stay with me. The doctor said he knew it was wearing them out, but that if I insisted on being out of Intensive Care, I had to agree to having someone around at all times. I know my family was glad I was feeling better, and I don't think they minded staying with me, but I'm sure they were wondering why I couldn't have just stayed in the ICU so they wouldn't have to take time from work to sit with me.

The reason — although, they never thought it was a very substantial one — made sense to me: I was going to get better and there are certain steps to getting better, one of them being moving out of Intensive Care. Besides, my new room was huge, and I decided it would be perfect for setting up my temporary office.

I set it up just like an office, too. I had all my wallpaper books, fabric books, and all kinds of design supplies there so I could show my workers what I needed them to do when they came in.

While I tried my best to run the business from my bed, I was also working on the March of Dimes booth. It took me about four months just to plan it out. I had one of my designers draw a big tunnel with a little light at the end of it and a wheelchair coming through the tunnel.

"When she first started the actual construction of the March of Dimes project, I had to scurry around and get material for her," Betty remembers. "I was always running my legs off, bringing her stuff to the hospital."

After I had completed the booth, I started designing the dress

I was going to wear to the March of Dimes gala to which I had been invited.

"I was thrilled that she wanted to design her dress when she couldn't even stand up," Betty recalled.

Betty may have been thrilled, but the six nurses and technicians that had to hold me up while I was being measured were far from happy. They didn't want me designing the dress or even going to the gala, and they were quick to tell me what they thought of it. I just wish they could have seen the dress. It was gold and silver with a wide sash and two big rosettes — very fancy. They would have been impressed.

But they were never very happy with me. I had two telephones set up in the room, and whenever someone would call and ask for me, the nurses would say, "Of course she's here! She operates this paradise!"

"Dorris always got the nurses to help her out, no matter how much they disapproved of what she was doing," said Betty. "They transcribed lists of things for each of us to do since Dorris still couldn't write. I think they became friends."

In the five months I was in the hosptial, I got to know all the doctors and nurses, learning their names and personalities. There was always someone stopping by to talk to me. Many of them liked to discuss GBS with me, and I would ask them all sorts of questions about the treatments and recovery while they asked me about its effect on me. And the more I talked to them, the more I realized how lucky I'd been.

I hadn't realized how many GBS patients suffered from problems with their bodily functions. Nor had I realized just how close I'd come to losing control of my functions. The reason the doctors had kept me under such close supervision when I'd first checked into the hospital had to do with the likelihood of my rapid deterioration. Almost all patients who have just been diagnosed with Guillain Barré are closely monitored for infections and the typical complications with heart rate, blood pressure, bowel control, breathing and swallowing.

Since doctors usually observe GBS patients in the emergency room, they are prepared to treat anything that creates a medical emergency. There may not be a tried-and-true treatment for Guillain Barré Syndrome, but there is a whole slew of preventive and supportive treatments for the complications of Guillain Barré, which can be life-threatening and create the real dangers of the disorder.

I learned from the medical staff members that there are medications used for regulating a patient's heart rate, blood pressure and bowels. But they said that most of the treatments involve tubes that connect patients to whatever device it is that they're dependent upon. For the patients who've lost bladder control, for example, a tube called a catheter is set in the bladder and serves to drain the urine. Or, if the patient can't swallow, nutrition is provided through the nasagastric tube, which is stuck up through the nose and into the stomach. These patients will also require a ventilator and, more than likely, fluids and drugs will have to be infused directly into their veins.

Perhaps the most terrifying complication of Guillain Barré is the weakened muscles that control breathing and coughing. While my respiratory muscles had weakened, I still hadn't ever required a ventilator, as about a third of all GBS patients do. That isn't to say that this complication isn't important; it's definitely the difficulty that creates the most concern. For patients who can't breathe on their own, the ventilator and the heart monitor become their most critical support. The heartbeat is monitored and the pulse is recorded from the electrocardiogram that appears on a video screen. The data on the screen also lets the doctors locate any problems that might require more attention.

When a patient is connected to a ventilator, the doctors first perform a tracheotomy. In other words, they make a hole in the windpipe so that they can stick a tube into the airway. This tube is then attached to the mechanical ventilator.

In addition, they insert another tube called an endotracheal tube in the throat of the patient, which keeps the fluid in the mouth and the acid in the stomach from going down the wrong tube and into the lungs. The thing is, this tube can only be left in the throat for two weeks. If the patient still needs assistance breathing, doctors will make a tracheostomy, which is different than a tracheotomy and which is just a little hole in the middle of the neck. It goes into the windpipe and it allows the patient respiratory assistance for as long as he needs it. Although I couldn't imagine it, many patients have told me that it's pretty comfortable!

If patients are put on ventilators, they must regularly have the congestion sucked out of their lungs so that they don't acquire pneumonia. I spoke with a patient who had been taken off a ventilator the week before. She said that the congestion had been one of the worst parts about the process.

"I didn't like any part about it," she said, "but I would rather have tubes coming out of my head forever than to have to wake up and get my lungs vacuumed every morning. Immediately after the tracheotomy, my throat filled up with this disgusting red and green slime. That stuff didn't stop oozing until I was off the ventilator again. It was really gross."

Once the patient's breathing muscles are capable of working on their own, doctors take the tracheostomy tube out. They say it doesn't hurt and that the hole closes up pretty quickly, leaving just a small scar.

The doctors that I grilled for every little detail about treatment and recovery had to repeatedly remind me that I needed to learn to trust them.

"You're never convinced," Dr. Hecht laughed one day when he was trying to tell me that I needed to rest more. I had just got through telling him that I needed to demand more of myself.

"Those books can't tell me what my own body needs," I told him. "I know I need to keep running my business or I might go bankrupt and I'll surely go insane from boredom. This is one of those times when you've got to make yourself happy and motivate yourself. Sleep, more important than happiness? I'm not convinced."

Dr. Hecht just shook his head and smiled at me. "You look like any other patient, all propped up in that bed," he said. "But I'll be darned if I ever had any patient like you!"

I always enjoyed chatting with all the different doctors — and there must have been ten of them working on my case. I once asked Dr. Blake why I had so many doctors working with me, and he said that that was typical in GBS cases.

"The neurologist, the surgeon, the physiotherapist – they're all doing something different," he said.

"Don't forget the general practitioner," I reminded him.

"That's right," he smiled warmly. "We're everywhere."

There are so many different complications and treatments involved in Guillain Barré Syndrome, that it really was necessary to have each one of the doctors — at least at some point in the recovery.

While some doctors stand in the *Get Ready!* position and wait for a respiratory or cardiac emergency, others center in, concentrating only on the prevention of complications.

There was, for example, a doctor who was not, mind you, a physical therapist, but who visited me regularly to move my arms and legs up and down and to bend my knees and my elbows. She said that this was a technique that would keep my joints from getting stiff and prevent a condition called contracture in which the joints actually bend the wrong way.

"It also helps prevent bedsores," she told me. "But with this big fancy bed, I guess we don't have to worry too much about bedsores, do we?"

She was right; I did have a fancy bed. It was a preventive treatment in and of itself. Not only did it help prevent bedsores, but it also helped keep my legs from swelling. I've heard a lot of patients say that they had to wear special tights to get rid of the fluid that had accumulated in their legs. That, however, was something I avoided thanks to that fancy bed.

There are all sorts of complications that result from being paralyzed and, therefore, bedridden. The blood flow, for example, slows down significantly in the veins of the pelvic area and of the legs.

Because this could result in clotting and the passage of the clots to the lungs, my doctors gave me blood-thinners to prevent clots from forming in the veins.

I had learned how to use the bed from my physiotherapist, who began visiting me right after my last plasmapheresis. She'd come in and massage my hands and my feet, and then she'd move my knees, ankles, shoulders, elbows and wrists around in a circular motion. Then, just like the other doctor did, she'd move my arms and legs all around. The physiotherapist, however, said she was keeping my muscles flexible and strong. I wondered how my arms could possibly be flexible if I couldn't even feel them and how my legs could possibly be strong if they couldn't even hold me up.

Despite that confusion, I was excited about physical therapy. I remember being so impatient to get out of the hospital and into the rehab center, where, I imagined, I would actually be able to see my progress. I always liked to hear the therapists talk about their other patients who were relearning how to walk, how to tie their shoes, or how to make a bed. Those stories were motivating and inspirational for me, and, at times, I saw my recovery time and my future progress as an exhilarating prospect.

I asked a lot of questions about the therapies I would be involved with and their benefits. As I listened to the doctors describe the various exercises that I could expect to be doing, I noticed that the more enthusiasm I had about my rehabilitation, the more enthusiasm they had about their careers. It made me happy to watch these doctors as they reminded themselves of the reasons that they'd chosen their professions.

"She's the kind of patient that the staff wants to spend personal time with," Dr. Blake said. "Getting to know her more as a person, versus just as a medical case, was very easy to do with Dorris because she was so open and so positive. Most doctors won't tell you this, but doctors kind of have a tough exterior and a soft interior and they are affected by how the patients do. They are affected by patient's attitude. When a patient is sick and their attitude is poor, it's tough. When you have somebody who is sick, but their attitude is exceptional, it enthuses the whole staff.

"Dorris is a high energy kind of person," Dr. Blake said. "Her having that plus-positive sparky attitude was instrumental in getting her better than what she might have been if she didn't have that personality. It allowed her to get further along quicker with this disease. That's a personality trait. Whether you believe that people are born with that, or that they developed it early in life, that's something that helped her more than anything that the doctors did."

Most victims eventually shift from denial to acceptance. But I took a different route. When I got over my denial, I did accept that I had a problem, but I never accepted that the disease belonged to me. I never accepted that I would have it for the rest of my life and I did more than hope I would get better. I knew it!

Chapter Five:

Pushing Past the Limits

I CAN HONESTLY SAY that if I hadn't had the attitude I did, my recovery would have been a lot slower and probably less complete. My determination was the deciding factor for the doctors to allow me to move out of the hospital and into rehabilitation. I had been in the hospital for five months when Dr. Jeffrey Hecht came into my room and told me that I had graduated to the Patricia Neal Rehabilitation Center in the same building.

"What do you think, Dorris?" Dr. Hecht asked me. "Do you think you're ready?"

Was I?! He knew he didn't have to ask. I would have transferred my third week in the hospital if they would have allowed me, but I knew that there were certain things patients were supposed to be able to do before they were approved for a move to the rehabilitation center.

For example, they were supposed to have shown improvement when given the serial nerve conduction, velocity, and electromyography (NCV-EMG) test, which electrically reports whether the activity of the nerves and muscles has changed. I don't know what my results were on that, but I knew that most patients must be able to use the bathroom and feed themselves before they were considered for rehabilitation. I couldn't yet pass either of those tests. I didn't even have feeling! But I didn't want them to give it a second thought, so I didn't ask why they were letting me transfer. It wasn't until much later that I learned that the decision had been based on my attitude.

Of course, I didn't care why they were allowing me to transfer so early. I was more than ready to go. I had heard wonderful things about the Patricia Neal Rehabilitation Center, and I was sure that once I was there, it would be a matter of weeks before I was able to walk again. Twenty-one years ago, the center was named for Patricia Neal, an Oscar-winning actress from Knoxville who suffered a massive stroke when she was pregnant at the age of thirty-two. She is an amazing woman and because she wanted to continue acting, she was determined to get past her debilitation. Although I am no actress and never have wanted to be, I was determined to follow in her footsteps and get past my paralysis. I knew that at least I had to try.

So, I went into the rehabilitation center with the same optimism I'd had in the hospital. I knew I was going to be working hard there, and I was willing to do everything necessary. I wanted to reach my highest potential, and I knew that I'd never get there unless I set that as my goal. Without it, I would have been lost.

The Patricia Neal Rehabilitation Center sees about five GBS patients a year. That isn't a whole lot, so they were very interested in my condition. They observed me twenty-four hours a day and they made extensive reports about my condition. There were all sorts of therapists and doctors coming to meet me, and they seemed to think I was going to need a speech therapist and a psychologist. It didn't take them long to realize neither were necessary in my case.

It was very conscientious of them to offer these professionals since, in many cases, both are very important. Psychologists are especially important for patients who are overwhelmed by their paralysis and the other problems that come along with it, such as dependency and loss of income. I met a lot of frustrated, depressed, and angry people while I was at the rehabilitation center, and it's certainly not hard to understand why.

Many patients pity themselves or are in denial. I have always been able to see the bright side of things, but it's not as easy for a lot of people. Attitude is so important in recovery and anyone having a negative emotional reaction to their condition should take advantage of the opportunity to talk to a psychologist, since most rehabilitation centers do offer them.

When I first got to the center, I naturally wanted to know everything about rehabilitation for GBS patients, and I made sure I found out. The most common answer I got was the importance of pacing myself.

"You must tell us when you start feeling tired or you feel like you've reached your peak for the day," the doctors would tell me. "This could be a long haul and you don't want to relapse or burn out your muscles."

But I'd already figured that out, and I was ready to know more. I wanted to be able to tell the therapists what I needed from them and I knew better than to assume they already knew. GBS is a very personalized condition; hence, the rehabilitation must be equally individualized. Based on the reactions I'd witnessed, I was sure that the staff at Patricia Neal Rehabilitation Center had never dealt with someone like me. I did some more research — this time to find out what the most important things were to tell my caretakers. The best advice I can offer is to ask questions and do research. You cannot be a passive survivor.

As it turns out, the recommendation that the doctors and nurses were giving me was the advice most stressed in all the material I'd seen. Everything I read said to take it slowly. Most rehabilitation patients are encouraged to exercise as much as they possibly can, but Guillain Barré Syndrome patients are told to move at a slow pace because excessive exercise can cause painful cramps and muscle exhaustion — even relapse. But there were a lot of other pieces of advice and information that I got from my reading as well.

First of all, I learned that if a GBS patient is weak enough to be put in a rehabilitation center, it can take anywhere from a few weeks to three years for them be able to regain normal functions. In addition, some of the rehabilitation can take place at home. I decided then and there that I was going to fall in that "few weeks" category, and that I'd be going home to do most of my rehabilitation. Lots of patients are still being treated for medical complications while they're in rehabilitation, and, since I wasn't being treated for anything except an occasional pain, I felt certain that I wouldn't need to be there too long.

I also learned that it was normal to have many doctors and therapists working with me. In fact, often several groups of professionals will work together to help GBS patients return to a relatively normal lifestyle. While there is usually one specialist in rehabilitation medicine who oversees the entire team, there is also an occupational therapist who gives instructions for the exercises that focus on strengthening the upper limbs, and a physical therapist who oversees the lower limb exercises. The occupational therapist teaches the patient to do things that are usually taken for granted, such as holding and manipulating things with your hands and arms. The physical therapist ultimately teaches the patient to walk.

It is also common for rehabilitation centers to have several nurses, interns, and neurologists working with GBS patients. It made me feel better to know that the reason there were always so many people observing me didn't have anything to do with my particular case or the amount of help I needed; it was simply a reflection of how specialized these people were in their particular crafts. They were all going to help me with whatever it was they were best at, and the general emphasis would be regaining the use of my weak muscles.

It was exciting to learn about the ways the different exercises are used as a patient progresses. There are exercises for every muscle. To strengthen the muscles in the hands, for example, oc-cupational therapists put a rubber band across the patient's fingers and the patient spreads his fingers apart over and over again. Even though I couldn't get my hands out of fist form and I couldn't even touch my thumb to my forefinger, it still amazed me that something that simple was an exercise. But it was and proved to be really difficult for me.

Other exercises seemed more usual and familiar, such as those done with weights on the mats. The only difference there is that the patient's goal is to lift his ankle, whereas that would seem like relaxation to most people. I was beginning to realize how much work was going to have to go into my rehabilitation. I had no idea it was going to be that hard!

The ways that therapists re-teach patients to walk fascinated me. Some patients are put in therapeutic pools with warm water, because the water helps relieve the stress on their muscles. Then, once the patient has a little bit more strength in his legs, he uses equipment like parallel bars, walkers, crutches, or canes for support and balance while he practices walking. And then, eventually, he can walk again on his own.

The whole point of rehabilitation is that the patients relearn to move the muscles they need to function normally and that they do this without relying on only the strongest of their muscles. The other major focus in the rehabilitation of GBS patients is not to strain the muscles. Since rehabilitation for Guillain Barré Syndrome is extremely individualized, everything I learned from my research told me that I should ask even more questions to make sure I was getting the most out of my therapy and to find out which exercises were best for me. I should be outspoken about what I felt worked and what wasn't. *Well*, I thought, *that part won't be a problem!*

Since I still didn't have any feeling, my rehabilitation began with the basics. The first specialist to help me, therefore, was the massage therapist. It was like living at a spa except that I couldn't feel the relaxing sensation most people do when they're being massaged. They pulled my fingers apart and massaged my hands and my feet and, one time, they even cut my toenails for me! When I first got to the rehabilitation center, I wanted to try everything at once. I thought the massage therapy was a waste of time — I wanted to move! It wasn't long, however, that I realized that I had to start somewhere, and that I should take it one step at a time and work with what I had, knowing it wouldn't be long.

"I can't get to the bathroom on my own now," I told the nurse one day as she was getting me ready for my shower, "but you just give me a week or two."

I imagine she was glad to hear that. I'm sure she didn't enjoy rolling me onto a sheet, lifting me onto the machine, and rolling me into the bathroom for my showers. For awhile they didn't even give me showers because, they said, if you try to lift someone who is paralyzed, you're liable to break their bones. Soon, as I was getting somewhere, they decided that I was finally strong enough for a shower. Or perhaps they couldn't stand the smell anymore!

I'd been in Patricia Neal Rehabilitation Center for about a month when I first got some feeling back in my shoulders. The doctors were shocked, and I was ecstatic. Soon after, I felt some tingling in my hands and I eventually started to feel the numbness in my feet. There were always people there watching me and there was always a big celebration whenever I announced a new sensation.

I'll never forget what it was like to move my finger for the first time. I'm not sure how long I'd been there at that point – time had begun to mean nothing to me — but it was just as I started to feel frustration setting in and I was having a hard time calming down because I wanted to do something so badly. And when my finger finally moved, it was like a promise: just a little longer. It was a wonderful feeling, but then again, it was a terrible feeling. The pain was unbelievable.

"That determined little cuss," I heard the doctor saying out in the hall after he'd seen what I had done. "She's already moved her finger!"

In some ways it was like I'd been in a strait jacket for years and years and it was finally being loosened. Although it had only been lifted from one of my fingers, I was finally emerging. I was coming out of this thing and I knew then that I was making some definite progress.

"Even minimal things, such as a twitch in a finger, she saw as progress," Dr. Blake said later. "She dwelt on the positive and not the negative, and that's why she got so much better than I'd have ever thought she could."

From that point on I was able to move a little more. Every day I saw a little bit of progress. And every day I got more and more eager to get out of there.

"I can walk a little," I told the doctor one day.

"How in the name of God can you get on the floor and try to walk when you have absolutely no use of your feet, or even your hands?" the doctor said.

"Just let me try," I pleaded.

The doctor told me it was against the law for him to allow me to do something like that at that point. Besides, he had said I could break an arm or a leg, which would mean it would take even longer for me to get better.

But I didn't care. I was determined to get out of that bed. And I decided to try it on my own, despite the warnings. So, one day I asked the nurse to tie my sheet to the bars on my bed.

He looked at me kind of strangely, but he didn't ask me why. I'd been sure that he would ask me, and I still wonder why he didn't. What must he have been thinking? But he must not have thought much of it because he just tied it up in a knot and left me alone.

Once he was gone, I used my arms to move myself over to the

end of the bed, and then, using the sheet as a slide, I propelled myself down onto the floor. And, of course, I fell as soon as I did it.

"What in the devil are you doing on that floor?" the nurse asked when he came in and found me lying on the floor.

"What's it look like? Trying to get out of bed."

"Dorris, Dorris, Dorris," he sighed. "You're going to break a leg."

He called in the technicians to put me back in bed and put higher bars up on it.

"That Dorris," I heard one of the doctors saying. "She'll try anything. It's like trying to cage up a wild animal."

That's exactly how I felt about my paralysis – like it was trying to cage me and I was the irrepressible animal. I was willing to do anything and everything to get past it, and I truly felt like I was accomplishing something by at least trying to get out of bed. I knew it was my goal and that there was a lot that still had to be accomplished before I could do it, but I wanted to try. Besides, they were always telling me that the more you move around, the sooner you're going to get better.

It was my determination that kept me going through it all. There were some good days and there were some really awful ones, but I wasn't willing to give up just because one day didn't go as well as I'd planned. Rehabilitation is like a roller coaster ride and there was no reason to dwell on the downside of it. And trust me, there were plenty downsides!

I spent most of my time at Patricia Neal in more pain than I thought possible. It's not fun to have therapists pulling and tugging at you and trying to unlock the joints and loosen the muscles. I worked harder there than I've ever worked before.

There are many different kinds of therapists and they're all wonderful, but they all want to spend hour upon hour working with you. I'd get so tired, I'd beg them to leave me alone, and that's not something I thought I'd ever do. But if you're not willing to work hard, Patricia Neal Rehabilitation Center is the wrong place to go; if you don't care how hard you have to work as long as you can walk out of there one day, you're in the right place.

Willpower is an important factor in rehabilitation for GBS patients, because unless you just keep on going, you'll never get over it. You have to face your day and get through your routine and, most importantly, always keep your goal in mind.

Believe me, I could not wait to reach my goal. But recovery from GBS is a slow process. In fact, **Getting Better Slowly** is the motto for the Guillain Barré Syndrome Support Group of the United Kingdom. Their mascot is the turtle. It had taken only a few days for me to become completely paralyzed, but it took seven months to move again, and there was no telling how long it was going to be before I was able to function normally. I've heard people say that GBS comes on like a lion and leaves like a lamb, and they were right. It took me a long time to accept it, but once I did, I decided to work with that and try to speed up my recovery as much as I could.

Still, it was quite a while before I could really work my fingers back and forth or touch the tips of my fingers with my thumb. I think it was squeezing a rubber ball that really started rebuilding the strength in my hands. Before long they were trying to teach me how to cook.

I'm not too big on cooking, and I told them I wasn't interested in learning how to do it, but they said it was the movement that my hands would be making, not the food itself, that was important. So, for the first time in my life, I made a pizza. It was hard enough for me to take a knife and spread mayonnaise on a slice of bread, and there I was making a pizza!

But I did it. I was willing to try everything, and I resolved to do everything in my power to get out of there. I was still trying to run my business from my bed, and the more I did that, the more I realized I had to get out of there and get to work. I did everything I set my mind to and almost everything my therapists told me to do. There were certain steps that the therapists wanted me to take, much like the various steps that one teaches a child, and some of those steps I liked. For example, working with a big rubber ball — lying on a mat and lifting it with my legs.

The leg exercises were always the hardest for me — those and an exercise in which you have to roll over, but I could tell they were helping. Everything helps, which is not to say I enjoyed it all. Take the "nuts & bolts" exercise, for instance. The therapists would help me up onto a platform, and I had to balance up there while I was supposed to put some little nuts onto different sized bolts. It wouldn't have been as tiring as it was if they didn't make me do it twenty-five times a day!

Not only were the exercises were tiring, but the everyday activities of life were, too. I had to relearn everything. It was like being a child all over again, except more frustrating, because I could remember how easy things like brushing my hair, picking up a book, writing a check, and tying my shoes had been only a few months ago. Now they felt like impossible tasks. I couldn't even do voluntary things, like turning over in bed. I remember the first time I rolled over in bed. It felt like the most miraculous and exciting thing that ever happened to me.

But when it came to the everyday things like spooning food into my mouth and brushing my teeth — things that I now had to think about doing — I needed a lot of practice. I was irritated that I couldn't do such simple tasks, and my therapist would remind me over and over that some GBS patients, like those on respirators, have to relearn to breathe and how to talk. I knew I was lucky in that regard, and I was constantly thanking God for keeping me from that situation. But still, I was frustrated.

It wasn't until a therapist gave a demonstration at the Center that I got any input on how to make these tasks easier for myself. He showed us several little tools that help people who are recovering from paralysis do everyday things, like making sandwiches and cutting cheese. After the demonstration he passed out a catalog. Apparently this catalog was put out by the rehabilitation center, but no one had ever shown it to me or even mentioned these tools. So I had to ask for them for myself. They really were some of the handiest supplies for people trying to get on with their lives after paralysis or similar handicap.

I ordered an apparatus to help me button and zip my clothing, and when I used it I felt like a new person. I could finally dress myself! All I had to do was hook this wire around the button or the zipper and pull, and I was dressed. It was a perfect little gadget, and I used it for about a month and a half, until I was able to do it on my own. I urge patients to ask about special tools. Often, they have the supplies, but they neglect to offer them to patients. And it is a wonderful feeling to be able to do a few things for yourself.

Another thing that helped me was a toothbrush with a big sponge around its handle to make it easier for gripping. I didn't find out about that until one day when I insisted on brushing my own teeth. I'm very particular about things like that, and I just wasn't happy that I couldn't brush my own teeth. One day I decided that I was going to do it, no matter what it took.

"Dorris," my doctor said, "you can't do that."

"Well," I said, "I'm going to do it. You just hold on a minute while I think of a way to do it."

While I was thinking about it, my doctor had a bright idea, and he wrapped a big sponge onto the neck of the toothbrush and secured it with a rubber band. It was perfect because it actually fit into my hand and I could brush my own teeth.

Creative tools like these are very important because they help patients feel accomplished and successful. It can be pretty overwhelming when you realize that you can't do anything for yourself and you're going to have to relearn everything. So every little thing that you can do for yourself makes you feel a little bit better about yourself, which is what most disabled people need.

There are other things the disabled require, including the opportunity to talk to people in similar situations. For someone who is paralyzed, it can be hard to believe that doctors and therapists — who have full use of all their muscles — can possibly understand what you're going through. Four GBS patients came and talked to me when I was first admitted to the hospital, and because of the positive outlook I have on my recovery, the doctors thought it would be a good idea for me to talk to some of the depressed patients in the Rehabilitation Center. My room often felt like Grand Central Station with all my doctors, nurses, therapists, employees and, now, other patients.

Once, a nurse who had suffered a stroke came to see me. "I can't believe you feel like you do," she said when she saw that I was conducting business from the room.

"It's never as bad as it seems," I told her. "The worst part is that you have to waste so much time getting back to where you were. But really, you'll feel better in no time. Just be thankful for what you've got."

She smiled an unconvincing smile and looked at me in disbelief. But every time I saw her after that she thanked me. "I haven't stopped looking on the bright side since I talked to you," she told me once. "There are a lot of things that could have happened that didn't happen."

And she was right. There were so many things that she, and everyone else, for that matter, could have lost. If they were in the Patricia Neal Rehabilitation Center, there was a good chance that their improvement was imminent, and I made sure to remind people of that.

I talked to all sorts of people with all sorts of disabilities. It was always hard to talk to the young kids that they brought to my room. One seventeen-year-old tennis player had been torn all to pieces, and his legs and arms were paralyzed by a car wreck. It had been his birthday, and he'd decided to go down to the strip to drink with his friends. Understandably, he was devastated, but I advised him that dwelling on the negative aspects would only hinder his recovery.

"What's done is done," I told him. "It's what isn't done that you should be concentrating on now."

A few months later I saw him taking some steps with the physical therapist. "You were right," he said. "You changed my thinking, and I'll never forget you."

"Just take one day at a time," I reminded him. "Today might not be too good, but tomorrow will be beautiful."

It felt good to be able to lift these patients' spirits, and it lifted my own to be able to do it. But then the doctors threw me some curve balls: they started sending me terminal cancer patients. Although it was a little bit harder for me to give these people encouragement and instill hope, it was just as easy to remind them of the importance of faith. Most of them were obviously scared. I told some of them about my encounter with Jesus and the incredibly wonderful feeling that had come over me.

"There is no reason to be scared," I assured them. "It was the most comforting place I'd ever been. I would have gladly gone with Jesus had that been His intention. You've got to have faith that He will take you when He is ready, and that should greatly excite you because I can promise you this: you've never been anywhere like that before."

It got to the point where, as soon as they brought people into Occupational Therapy and Physical Therapy the doctors would say, "Don't worry. We'll go wake Dorris up and she'll make you feel better."

If there weren't patients talking to me in my room, that meant that the doctors had sent me to the patients' rooms to give them pep talks. Even at the dinner table in the dining hall, my table was always full of patients wanting to talk to me.

"Dorris has a powerful effect on other patients," Dr. Blake said. "It's always good for someone who's been there to talk to patients, especially when the person who has already been through it has the type of attitude that Dorris does. She is able to remind people that they can only get better and to allow people to call upon the resources they have inside them to battle whatever they have. It does make a difference to have someone reminding you not to get down on yourself, that the sun is going to shine tomorrow."

I even talked to some outpatients who were recovering from GBS. One woman, who could do almost nothing for herself, was always telling me how frustrating it was that her parents had to run her house for her.

"They've already raised me," she said. "It's so unfair to them."

"Do what you can," I said. "They don't mind helping you out because parents like to feel needed. Plus, they know better than you do that it won't be long until you won't be needing them anymore. Have faith."

And she did because it wasn't long that she walked into my room to tell me that her parents had finally moved back to their own house and that she was able to do almost everything on her own. "I even cooked a three-course meal last night," she said.

There was another outpatient who seemed to always be hanging around. I'd thought for a long time that he was an inpatient. When I found out that he didn't have to be at the Center, I went over and asked him why he wasn't at home doing something he wanted to do.

"It just doesn't seem like my home anymore," he said. "I don't feel safe there."

I thought about that and I understood what this man was saying. I saw how that could happen. After all, it always feels a little strange to come home after being away for an extended period. I remember it taking me a couple of days to feel comfortable again when I got home from business trips that were as short as a week long. At that point, I'd been gone for almost a year!

I talked to one of the nurses about what the man had said, and I asked her if that uncomfortable, lost feeling was common with patients that had been in the hospital for long periods of time.

"Oh yeah," she said. "The psychologist deals with that issue a lot. But that's one reason we have the Sunday visit program."

"The what?" I'd never heard of such a thing.

"Once you're approved to do so, you can go home on Sundays after breakfast. Just as long as you're back by five. You're probably eligible to do it," she said. "Ask Dr. Hecht about it."

"Oh, I will," I assured her.

As soon as Dr. Hecht came into my room that day, I started pleading for him to let me go home for a Sunday. "Please," I said, "I know I can do it. I'll just go to my sister's. She'll take care of me."

After he'd listened to about ten minutes of my whining, Dr. Hecht laughed. "Dorris, you sound like a child begging for the toy that's already under the Christmas tree."

"What?"

"We've already decided that you're well enough to try out the Sunday program," he said. "We were going to tell you about it toward the end of the week so you wouldn't have so long to anticipate it."

"Really?" I said. "I get to go home for the day?"

"Not until Sunday, Dorris," he reminded me. "Be patient."

He didn't know how close Sunday sounded to me after thinking in terms of months for so long. Ecstatic, I spent the rest of the week making plans. I decided that I'd go to Naomi's house and then go to church with her and her husband, but I had a hard time deciding what I wanted to do after church; there were way to many things that I'd been unable to do for so long. In the past seven months I had probably started 1,000 sentences with the phrase, "As soon as I get out of here, I'm going to. . . ."

I knew it would be quite an experience leaving the hospital setting, and stepping — or, rather, wheeling — out into the real world after so long, but I was ready. Oh, how I was ready!

And then, after what seemed like a year, it was Sunday. Even though I hadn't gotten a wink of sleep due to the excitement, I got up around six o'clock that morning to try to fix myself up a little. About an hour later, Dr. Hecht came in and saw me lying in bed trying to put makeup on my face.

"What are you doing now, Dorris?" he asked.

"Any old barn looks better with a little paint on it," I told him.

"My heavens," he chuckled, "you *are* getting better if you're putting that war paint on."

Thirty minutes later, they strapped me into the hospital van and took me to my sister's. I stared out the windows and thought about how nothing had changed. I remember everything struck me as bright and vibrantly colored. When we arrived at Naomi's house, they slid me out of the van, onto the board and into my wheelchair.

"Dorris! Where have you been?" my brother-in-law joked when he first saw me. "We thought you'd run off and eloped."

"Nope," I laughed. "I'm still single."

"Do you still want to go to church, Dorris?" Naomi asked. "Because we need to leave if you do."

"Well of course I want to," I said.

Naomi attends a very small church and it was hard getting through all the people, but everyone was very helpful and gracious. They even acknowledged me during the announcements. "Please welcome Dorris Wilcox, who has been in the hospital with Guillain Barré Syndrome for seven months. She was allowed to leave for the first time today, and she is here with us to celebrate the Lord," the preacher said.

After the service, a lot of people wanted to talk to me and tell me how happy they were to see me, but I was already beginning to feel worn out and I tried to keep the conversations brief. I'd done more in the past few hours than I'd done in the past few months, and it was starting to take its toll.

We returned to Naomi's, had a nice lunch and Mable Bell and Margaret came over to visit. However, I had not considered the problem needing to use the bathroom would present. I had a bedpan and everything, but I couldn't bend my knees to use it very well.

"What should I do?" I asked. "I don't want to make a mess."

"Go ahead and make a mess," Naomi said.

"But –"

"Make a mess this time, Dorris," my brother-in-law said. "By the next time you need to go, I'll have a little contraption for you." All three of us women looked at him with question marks on our faces. "You'll see," he laughed. "Go now! I don't want you making a mess in here!"

Naomi brought me to the bathroom and, between the two of us, we were able to keep it reasonably clean in there. When we came out of the bathroom, Naomi's husband was gone.

"Where. . . ?"

Margaret and Mable Bell just shrugged. When he reappeared, he wanted to take the bedpan off somewhere. "Yeah, go ahead," I smiled. "Naomi washed it out."

"What a nut!" Naomi said, shaking her head.

But she, nor I for that matter, had any idea just what he was doing out there with my bedpan. And, when he returned with his invention about an hour later, our expressions turned from amusement to applause.

He had built a plywood platform with a little shelf on it. To demonstrate how it worked, he put the bedpan on the little shelf and showed me that now all I had to do was slide from my wheelchair and onto the platform. The bedpan was positioned so that I could use it easily without bending my legs.

"What do you think?" he asked me proudly. "You think I can get a patent on it?"

"I don't know about a patent," I said. "But you've definitely got my two-thumbs-up. This is brilliant."

He beamed like a little boy. Naomi told me that any time they have people over, he brings out the contraption to show it off.

My son, Mike, brought me to Naomi's, and the hospital van came and picked me up around five. I was so tired by that time, I was glad to see it. The day's activity had worn me out and all I wanted to do was sleep. Besides, now that I knew I could leave the hospital on Sundays, I decided I'd go visit my family every weekend.

And, although I didn't make it every Sunday, I did go visit my sisters about six or seven more times while I was at Patricia Neal. I alternated between Naomi's, Margaret's, and Mable Bell's houses, and we'd go to church whenever I got there on time. We never really did much of anything — there were a lot of rules about what you could and couldn't do on Sunday visits and, besides that, I was usually pretty worn-out just from getting up and getting there. But it was fun for all of us, and I began anxiously awaiting my release from the rehabilitation center.

The months passed gradually and I was hard at work the entire time. Not only was I restoring my own body and the mindset of so many other patients, but I was also working tirelessly on the March of Dimes booth. When I'd finally finished the display booth, it looked like a beautiful home. I was extremely proud of it and when it won second place, I was beaming.

"If I'd been there to talk about it, it would have won first place," I told Betty. She had come by to tell me the news and to give me the invitation to the gala at the Hyatt Regency Hotel where they were going to present the prizes, and to the luncheon a month later.

It had taken a lot of convincing, but I eventually persuaded the doctors to allow me to go to the gala. I could hardly contain my excitement. I started getting ready for the event about four hours before Michael was supposed to pick me up. It had been so long since I'd been dressed up that I wanted to look especially nice. So I asked my niece to come do my hair and fingernails. She gave me artificial fingernails. Naomi brought over the dress that I had made for myself.

"How am I going to get pantyhose on?" I wondered out loud.

Naomi just looked at me and then went and got a couple of doctors to see if they had any suggestions. They looked at me like I'd lost my mind. One of them stood there for a few minutes and just scratched his head.

"Dorris, there are so many things we could be doing for you besides putting these pantyhose on," one of them said.

"Doctor," I said, "if you have any suggestions then you just come tell me, but I don't know of any others. This is a formal occasion and I'm going to have on pantyhose!"

They thought about it a little more, and then they finally decided that the nurses would have to hold me up and pull the hose onto my legs. What an ordeal! It took four nurses to get the things on me, but by the time it was time to go, I was all set.

When my son Michael arrived to take me to the hotel, they had to slide me out of my wheelchair and onto a slick wooden board about the size of a desk drawer to get into the car. But once I was in there, I didn't have any problems.

I met some friends and a whole bunch of my designers and decorators a the hotel. And, once they got me into the wheelchair and I'd asked Michael to pick me up in a couple of hours, the crew brought me inside.

The first person I saw when I arrived was Tennessee Congressman John Duncan and his wife.

"Dorris," his wife said, "you've done beautifully."

I beamed. It always feels good to be praised. As it turns out, I'd be getting more than my share of praise at that gala. People were delighted with the booth I'd designed, but I really think it was the fact that I'd done it from my hospital bed that impressed them most.

But the compliments were just part of the fun. The room was decorated beautifully and the food was delicious. Alice and Mary Holland were the designers. We had an exhilarating time.

The only problem I had was trying to figure out how to get the pantyhose off to use the bathroom. Betty, who had met me there, and two of the designers came into the stall with me to try to help. It was a riot! After ten minutes of tugging, interrupted by fits of laughter, we eventually pulled the hose off. And then we had to get them on again.

"Don't you dare wear hose to the luncheon next month," Betty warned.

Of course I did wear hose to the luncheon. It was much easier to get ready this time because I already knew how to do it. My sister brought over a few of my fancy dresses and I picked one from the selection. Then she did my hair and makeup and I was ready to go.

The luncheon was held at a beautiful house on Loudin Lake with two indoor swimming pools. I was in awe of the beauty of the home from the moment Michael pulled the car into the driveway. As soon as I'd reached the door and been rolled inside by one of the Knoxville news commentators, my awe grew. There were hundreds of guests, and the owner of the house hurried over to me and kissed my hand.

"Thank you so much for coming," he said.

"My pleasure," I said. "Trust me, it's better than sitting in the rehabilitation center all day."

I met the same crowd there that I had at the gala: Betty, and then about five of my designers and my decorators. They really were the most supportive group, taking me around the room while we ate anything we could get our hands on and had our pictures taken. We even got our pictures taken with Alex Haley, the well-known author of *Roots*.

"You've got it, girl," he said to me right after the flash. "I hope you know that."

"Yeah," I said. "I know I do. I just wanted to help. As long as I can help others, that's what I want to be doing."

And that's what I kept on doing. I'll never forget one of the last patients who came into my room at the Center. I had thought he wanted some help like the other patients who visited me, and maybe he did, but I couldn't be sure. He started telling me about how, eight years ago, he had had GBS, and how ever since then he had been fine, except for a bothersome tendency to drop things.

"But now I've got that same numbness in my legs that you get when it's first hitting, you know?"

I nodded. That's not a feeling you can easily forget.

He went on to say that he's been losing his balance and falling a lot. "For a while my face was getting numb again, and sometimes my right arm and my back go numb. But that comes and goes — usually with stress. When it gets really bad, I can't see right, and I feel like I'm inside a fishbowl. When I get like that, I just lie in bed and wait for my body to stop buzzing. But any little noise or movement hurts me so much I feel like jumping out of my skin. It's exactly like it was eight years ago," he said, "only it's worse because I thought I'd never have to deal with it again."

This may have been the hardest patient I ever talked to. Not because his situation was any worse than anyone else's and not because he was more depressed than anyone else, but because this was something I had neither dealt with nor even considered. No one had ever told me that GBS could come back after eight years, and that came as a shock to me. Also, I didn't know what this man wanted from me. He didn't sound upset about the relapse and he didn't seem hopeless; he just seemed to want me to know that this had happened to him.

I smiled up at him from my bed. "Well," I said, "are you ready to fight another battle?"

Chapter Six:
Fighting for Freedom

IF THERE'S ONE THING I learned about GBS, it's that it's one battle after another. Just when you've mastered one thing, you're faced with something else.

As eager as I'd been to get out of the Patricia Neal Rehabilitation Center, once I'd actually pleaded my way out and been approved to continue my therapy as an outpatient, I realized that this challenge — going home and trying to get on with my life — was going to be one of the biggest thus far. I knew it wouldn't be as bad for me as it was for as the man who had felt uncomfortable in his own home, but it was definitely going to be different than just going home for the day.

According to Dr. Blake, "Neurological disorders are very difficult to recover from, even with a good attitude."

When I started pestering the doctors to let me go home, they wanted to know who was going to take care of me and where I was going to live.

I'd already thought the whole thing out, and I told them how I'd told Michael that I needed him to take a year off from college to come take care of me. I didn't tell them, however, what Michael's reaction had been. "Mother," he'd said. "I'm not going to give up a year of school to come clean your tail!"

"Yes, you are," I said. "I cleaned yours and now it's your turn."

I knew this was not something Michael wanted to do, but I also knew that it was something that he was going to do. Some of the staff members wanted to talk to him before they made a decision about my release, and I told them that was fine. Then they went to see if my home had all the right facilities that I'd be needing. Not only did I need wheelchair access, they said, but I also needed to have an easy passage between the bedroom and the kitchen.

I remember being delighted with the prospect of going home and moving past my illness. But the closer it came to the time that I was actually going to be set free, the more apprehensive I became. After all, I'd been protected by professionals for eight months, and now it was time for me both to protect myself and prove to myself that all that effort had been worth it. I wasn't actually scared, but I was definitely worried.

It didn't take me long to realize that I was hardly going to be on my own. Everyone wanted to help. Some of the local churches had filled my cupboards with groceries, and my sisters were always helping me out with cleaning. I guess they know how particular I am about cleanliness and where I live because they washed my windows, scrubbed my porches and handled almost all the major cleaning. My designers were also very helpful. One of them stayed with me to take care of me and answer the phone for the first four and a half months.

Not only were people more than willing to help out, but the staff from the Patricia Neal Rehabilitation Center was also adamant about staying in control. They confined me to my house, forcing me to stay downstairs in the showroom and making me use a potty chair instead of the bathroom. I didn't mind staying in the showroom — they set up a bed in there and it looked like a bed for a princess — but I was not happy that I wasn't allowed to go to my own bathroom! This is my home, I fumed inwardly. I can go anywhere I please.

And I did, too. It took me three days, but I eventually figured out how to pull my wheelchair down the hallway and into the bathroom and then how to hoist myself, using the edge of the tub for support, up and onto the toilet.

A lot of people would crawl into bed and try to forget about what was going on around them. But not me. Even though the bed made me feel like a princess, I was determined not to be' confined there forever; I had to rebuild a life for myself. I wanted to start over.

The first step, I decided, was to move to a new home. A lot of things you read will tell you that it's best for Guillain Barré Syndrome outpatients — especially for those that are still in wheelchairs — to stay on one level, at least for a little while. But one article I read said that climbing stairs will help strengthen your leg muscles, and that made more sense to me. After all, I couldn't wait until I could walk again; I wanted to do everything possible to get better quickly.

I found a townhouse that would force me to go up twenty-four steps to get to the bedroom and rented it. My younger brother, J.D., took me to look at it and he must have called my sister to inform her of my decision because she immediately arrived at my house.

"Dorris, you're in a wheelchair! What are you doing?" she cried in disbelief and frustration

"I won't be in this thing long," I replied.

She gave me an exasperated look and picked up the telephone to call one of the doctors.

"You're not going to believe it," she told him. "Dorris has got herself a townhouse and all the bedrooms are upstairs." She handed me the phone right away, throwing me an "I told you so" look.

"Dorris, you cannot do this," the doctor said.

"I'm doing it," I said.

"Well, I'll just have to come out there on my lunch hour," he said.

"All right," I said, "but you'll need to come out here 'cause I'm moving and you need to help me."

He just about had a fit, but I moved anyway. My therapists and doctors said that, if I insisted on staying there, then I wasn't allowed to go upstairs. They fixed up a pallet on the couch downstairs and said that I had to sleep there, which of course didn't last long.

They hadn't so much as gotten into their car before I was crawling up the stairs one step at a time. I wanted to sleep in my bed and I refused to let anyone tell me otherwise. Although I understood their concern and willingness to help, I knew that doing things my way rather than theirs had proven highly beneficial so far.

On November 16, 1990, I received the Patricia Neal Award For Excellence for my outstanding recovery from a debilitating illness, further proving the efficacy of my manner in handling GBS. The award is presented annually to the person who has come the closest to resuming independent lifestyles after rehabilitation and, by that time, I was definitely independent.

"Dorris would get up and wash her own dishes," Betty recalls. "She'd roll over to the sink in her wheelchair and just pull herself up into a standing position next to the sink. And she still kept her house clean. She just learned how to do it all for herself, despite the fact that she couldn't walk."

Nevertheless, the rehabilitation center wouldn't let me be fully independent. There are certain steps everyone is required to go through as an outpatient to ensure that each person is strong enough to live on his own before they set anyone completely free. Physical therapists and nurses are usually part of the plan for outpatients.

The physical and occupational therapy is easy to continue

at home, although a lot of outpatients return to their rehabilitation center to continue their exercise programs. The activities of daily living — getting dressed, bathing, and cooking — are exercises in and of themselves. Still, therapists are effective in monitoring exercise, since one can easily encounter strain and muscle aches.

Since it's usually different for everyone, through trial and error, they can help you figure out how much you can work before you need to rest. I know a lot of outpatients also make use of social workers to help them relearn how to drive, find employment, and capitalize on the services for the physically impaired.

I didn't really need that kind of help; I could do those things on my own. I had to accept some kind of outpatient assistance, however, so I joined a support group and, after some persuasion from the social worker, I agreed to use a home health care service. I had no idea what I was getting into.

Home health care provides staff to come to your house with food, and do things like check your blood pressure, take your pulse, weigh you and bathe you. But it was a lot more like a circus; every hour or so, somebody else was knocking on the door, and I grew exceedingly aggravated by the interruptions. After about a week, I told them to stop bringing me food.

"This tastes like dog food," I said.

"Dorris," the nurse said. "Have you ever eaten dog food?"

"No, but I've seen dogs turn their nose up at it, so it must not be too good," I said. "Don't bring me any more food. I'll have the restaurant down the road deliver me good food from now on."

Then, after about two weeks, I stopped letting them come over to give me baths. I never liked them to do that and I told Michael that I needed his help.

"You?" he asked incredulously, knowing how independent I am. Even though he had moved in to help me, I seldom needed him.

"Yeah," I said, "I need you to call some of my decorators and figure out a way to get me showered without all those people coming over here."

"Well," he said. "Let me call Dr. Blake."

"Let me talk to him," I said when he'd gotten Dr. Blake on the phone. He handed me the receiver.

"Dr. Blake, I don't want these people coming over here to bathe me anymore. I want to take my own shower, and I want to be able to do it when I want to do it."

Dr. Blake said I could take my own shower if I had someone helping me. I asked Michael to install a chair in the tub, and my decorators helped me into the chair, but didn't improve matters much. There are some things you just don't want people helping you with. I knew I had to do something about it. I had to take charge.

I had my showerhead put on a cord to make it easier for me and not more than four days later, I'd figured out how to get from my wheelchair to the toilet and then swing myself over the toilet, into the bath and onto the chair without anyone's help. It was a wonderful accomplishment, and I knew I was going to be able to soon do it with ease.

Not long after that I got completely fed up with home health care and all the nurses constantly coming over to my house.

"This is ridiculous," I told my doctor hotly. A nurse had called him to complain about my failure to cooperate when I wanted to go for a ride with one of my friends. The nurse protested, saying I had to stay house-bound. "It's a waste of everyone's time. They do not need to be coming over here every day."

I eventually convinced them to change the home health care visits to once a week. It wasn't long until I told them to stop coming altogether. I was just too independent to let them help me.

I let the therapist at Patricia Neal help me three times a week for eighteen months to rebuild the muscles that had become so weak. She worked me very hard, but it was a tiring routine and there wasn't much variety to the exercises. Most of them were squats and stretches designed to help me stand up again.

Still, I didn't feel that I was really benefiting from the exercises she was prescribing me. I could tell which exercises would help and which wouldn't, but always seemed to get stuck doing the latter. I was determined to stand up and walk and that's all I thought about. I would do anything necessary to reach that goal. I wanted to try something new every day and constantly asked to try new exercises, but they kept telling me I wasn't advanced enough.

"How do you know?" I'd demand. "I haven't tried it."

I wanted to use a slow bicycle called the QuadRiser. It stretches out your arms, your legs and your hips, and although your muscles are moving, the bike is actually providing the power. The exercise was good for me because the paralysis had hit me hardest in the hips and spine.

Luke Bowman had invented the bike for his mother, who had a severe form of Alzheimer's disease. He had first invented it when I was still an inpatient at Patricia Neal. He came in to get feedback from patients who were using it, since it was the second he had invented. The first was designed for his father, who he was losing the use of his arms and legs. The bicycle had helped his father so much that Luke patented it and began selling it to rehabilitation centers and hospitals.

"Have you used the QuadRiser?" he asked me then.

"Me? Oh no," I said. "I'm not ready to use that."

"Oh, I think you can do it," he said. "It's easy."

I hadn't even moved at that point, and I was sure that I couldn't get on a bicycle.

"No," I said. "But it won't be long."

I told the therapist that I wanted to use it, but she told me I'd have to talk to the doctor about it. She said she couldn't allow me to do anything without his permission. So I talked to the doctor, and after he'd checked it out, he decided that I could use it for fifteen minutes at a time.

As soon as I got on the cycle, I could actually feel my muscles getting stronger as I used it. I used it for fifteen minutes, twice a day, three times a week for a long time. The therapists were amazed at my progress. It was a little bit difficult at first, but only a week later I was able to do it without any pain. Once I'd mastered it, I was ready to do it all.

When I finally felt like I'd gotten as much as I could out of the slow cycle, I moved on to the stationary bicycle. I could ride it for only five minutes at a time, but I still knew that it was helping.

I also continued to work with the occupational therapist at Patricia Neal. The muscles in my hands were still tight, but they had gradually begun to open up. I didn't like to use my time at the Center doing the painful hand exercises, since all it entailed was squeezing my fists a few times, which I could do at home.

One day one of the doctors called me to come in and after she had given me a good scorching, she asked, "Will you accept help from anyone?"

"I'll join a spa," I said.

Deciding that would be better than nothing, she warned me to pace myself, whatever I did. "Lots of exercises aren't safe or beneficial for the recovering Guillain-Barré patient," she told me. "It's easy to overexert your muscles and tendons, and that would only set you back."

When I joined the spa, I made sure to consult with the doctors there. When they started making suggestions for my exercises, however, they obviously didn't realize how far I'd already come. Every time they proposed an exercise, I would shake my head and say, "No, that doesn't help. I tried that already. I need something that will really build up my leg muscles."

They stood there and stared at me for awhile before they were able to make any more suggestions. I ended up working a lot on the weight bench and I felt that I was actually getting somewhere. With weights on my legs, I could feel the muscles gradually return to normal.

My good friend Art would often accompany me to Patricia Neal and to the spa. He had been a wrestler in college and he showed me the different exercises that he thought would get my legs moving and strengthen my back and spine. He also came with me to be supportive and keep me from going anywhere alone. Even when I had not been able to do an exercise satisfactorily, he always said that I'd done great.

"Don't worry," I'd tell him. "I'll do better next week."

"Just don't try to do something you're not ready to do," he'd warn. "Don't push yourself."

"You know I don't know what I can and can't do," I'd tell him. "I've got to try. You don't know if you can unless you try. And the more you try, the more you can do."

I was always finding something new that I could do now. I did whatever I set out to do. While my physical possibilities were expanding, however, my occupational probabilities were beginning to dwindle. After three months of trying, I finally realized that I wasn't going to be able to run my current business anymore. The phone was always ringing off the hook, and even though I had my designers there, the callers wanted to talk to me. It was just too much for me to handle right then.

On the other hand, I did need some kind of income. The bills had run up to over a half million dollars. I knew that if Andy Griffith had had to sell his entire art collection to pay the bills from his GBS attack, I was going to need help.

If there is one thing I cannot stress enough it is this: have good medical insurance. When they started demanding payments from me, I felt more helpless than I'd felt since the onset of Guillain Barré Syndrome. I didn't have any property to sell and I was too young for Medicare. I drew an annuity from the Navy, but I didn't think there was much else they could do for me.

Around that same time, someone from the University of Tennessee-Knoxville called me and asked me if I'd be interested in teaching Interior Design. I took them up on their offer and, even though I was still in the wheelchair, I taught the class. This not only gave me some income, but it also freed up some time so that I could get on the phone and begin hunting down services that provided assistance for disabled people.

Whenever I needed information, I always got on the phone and found the particular person who was in charge of whatever I need. I had learned that if you're naïve about something, the chances are that very few people know about it. Whoever you call doesn't care how naïve you are — they're going to tell you the answer. After I'd done a little research on the telephone, I found out that I was eligible for several benefits through the Tennessee Department of Human Services, and they were the first organization I called.

"Come on into the office and fill out some papers," the secretary said when I called.

"I'll come down there," I said, "but I can't fill out any paperwork. I can't even write. I'm still paralyzed."

"Are you sure you can get down here, then?" she asked.

"Oh yeah," I said. "I can get there."

As soon as I'd disconnected that line, I called two designers and asked them to come over and take me to the Human Services office.

Once we arrived, one of the designers went into the office and told them that they had to come get me because there hadn't been enough room in the car for the wheelchair, and I couldn't walk. Then, after a few minutes, a man came outside with a wheelchair and wheeled me inside to talk to the agents.

I wanted to know what they could do to help me, so I interviewed six or seven women. After the women had told me about the various organizations for which I was eligible and the services that they provide from which I could benefit, they took my hand, and helped me make an X to affirm that I wanted their help.

They told me that, under the Americans with Disabilities Act (ADA), I was eligible to use the C.A.C. LIFT, which is provided by the Knoxville Area Transit (KAT). For fifty cents a ride, the C.A.C. LIFT takes qualified people with disabilities all over the city. This is a wonderful service because it allows people in wheelchairs to go almost anywhere.

I urge people to advocate such a service in their hometown, because it makes disabled people a little less disabled. Simply by calling them, they will come, put you onto this lift and hoist you up onto the bus. It is very helpful, and I used it whenever I needed to go somewhere. That way, I was out running around town when I couldn't even walk!

Human Services offered me many services. They brought my medications to me when I called the prescriptions into the drugstore. The services are available; you just have to call to start receiving them. God was good to me: He didn't take my voice away, and that makes all the difference in getting assistance.

Because I didn't have the business to attend to anymore, I had a lot of free time to do all the things that I'd been missing out on. I spent more time with my friends. I hadn't been able to go shopping or go out to eat with them for so long.

Now, I'd often get tired in the middle of an outing and I'd have to stop. I know it was trying on my friends to deal with a handicapped person in public, but they were good to me.

"When we first started going out to eat, I had to cut her meat and feed her," Betty remembers. "She'd try to do it herself, and she didn't care when she dropped her food on herself in public. If anyone noticed she was making a mess, she would tell them she was recovering from Guillain Barré Syndrome, and then people wanted to help her. I admired her for not caring about what people thought of her."

Most people who noticed me wanted to know what was wrong and what Guillain Barré Syndrome was, and I was more than happy to tell them. GBS is something not enough people know about. If more people were aware of it and how it comes on like the flu, then they'd be able to stop it before it gets too far along.

Unfortunately, very few people realize what they're dealing with until it's already got the better of them. I wanted to spread the word that this disease is out there so if anyone I told happened to encounter it, they would be able to recognize it and get treatment. If just one person is a little bit better off because they listened to me talking about my experience, it's worth it to me.

"Dorris gave people courage," says Betty. "They'd see this lady who was supposed to be paralyzed from the neck down, trying to whip her paralysis, and they'd smile at her and ask her all sorts of questions. We'd go down the street, and there was Dorris, chattering like a magpie to everybody on the sidewalk. I don't care what anyone says, there are good people out there — people who want to help others — and I think they're attracted to Dorris.

"Whenever we were in town and we were having a hard time getting the wheelchair through a doorway or out of the car, or whatever, there was always someone who wanted to help. But sometimes Dorris was too proud to accept help and she'd struggle to get along on her own, and there was always a crowd watching her — cheering her on."

I wanted to go everywhere and do everything. It didn't matter that I was still in the wheelchair. I wanted to travel. It didn't take much convincing to get my friends to take a few trips with me. They were happy to go with me, and we went all over: South Carolina, Kentucky, Georgia, Virginia, and Florida.

It was great to feel like I was moving around again. I'd been confined to that hospital room for so long, it felt like a whole new world out there. I'd learned to work the wheelchair pretty well by then, and I encountered very few problems. I'd become primarily independent, and it felt great!

Although I had anticipated it might be somewhat different, my travels weren't that much different than the business trips I'd taken before I'd been hit with GBS. Ruth Jenkins Arnold, Al Smith, and his friend were especially good about taking me on trips with them. We went to the dog races every night in Florida, and when we went to the beach, they'd lift the wheelchair up and carry it through the sand. They even made me a little stepstool to help me get into their van.

My family never understood my love for travel. They had never traveled as extensively as I had, and every time I came back from a trip, they always wanted to see me. "It's always so quiet when you're gone," J. D. would tell me whenever I came back from a trip. "Not as much laughter."

Still, I didn't feel completely satisfied. There was something missing that running my decorating business had fulfilled for me. After all, I had spent most of my life making improvements in people's establishments, and I felt like I needed to find something that I could work at improving. I had been focused on improving my health for so long, and I wanted to do things for other people as well. It didn't take me long, however, to start noticing a lot of improvements that needed to be made in the way of handicapped accessibility.

My friends and I went to Charleston four times, and each time I noticed how hard it was to get around. Not because my friends weren't helpful — they did everything for me – but because South Carolina didn't have any laws about handicapped access or handicapped facilities.

"Dorris would have to go up stairs on hands and knees," Betty recalls. "Of course she couldn't use escalators either, with the wheelchair and all. But she always had a smile on her face. She never looked glum. She would just say, 'Here, you take my pocketbook,' and then she would crawl up stairs. To get down, she would sit down and scoot down on her bottom. This is the way you have to do it. People would look at her, smile, and ask her what her story was, and she would tell them. She was never embarrassed. She knew it was her illness and she knew she had to overcome it. But she also wanted to help other people overcome their disabilities."

I never really minded not being able to get around easily because I knew that I wasn't going to need facilities for the handicapped for long. It bothered me that there are so many people in wheelchairs for life, but it was nearly impossible for them to get around. That was something they would have to deal with for their whole lives. Anytime I noticed that there wasn't handicapped accessibility, handicapped facilities or even banisters on staircases, I would call a congressman in that state and ask him what could be done about it and to whom I needed to report.

I read in the newspaper that the South Carolina and Tennessee legislatures were going to pass bills that required public places to have handicap access and other features for disabled people. I wanted to understand the bill better, so I called the state General Assembly to talk to the some of the representative and senators. Actually, I knew all the South Carolina legislators by this time because I called to pester them about what needed to be done. Many times, I called them and they'd connect me to the White House within ten minutes.

It's my right to give my opinion to lawmakers, and it's the right of all Americans, but not enough people take the initiative to stand up for what they believe. There's no reason they shouldn't because not only is it easy, but government officials want to hear from the people. If you've got a voice at all, you can make a difference

When I was calling all those legislators to find out about the bill, they told me that it would require public places to be handicap accessible, meaning that they'd have to have ramps, handrails, larger bathroom stalls, lowered sinks and things of that nature. The bill also implemented some anti-discriminatory hiring policies for disabled people. As soon as they'd finished telling me about the bill, each of the legislators wanted to know what I thought about it. And I told them exactly what I thought.

If I — and hundreds of other handicapped people — hadn't called and badgered all those South Carolina officials about what needed to be done, they may have never come up with that bill. As of 1997, they passed it, mandating a law that requires all public places to be handicap accessible.

The more independent I became, the more I realized that I really needed some stable source of income. I was finally out of the wheelchair and although I still couldn't walk without my walker, I was a lot more mobile than I had been. I decided that it was time for me to start working again, and I seriously considered reopening my company.

In late 1991, when a friend of mine mentioned a beautiful house that was available in Pigeon Forge, Tennessee, I started thinking about opening a bed-and-breakfast like one I had renovated in Charleston. I called my friend and business associate, Art, to see what he thought about the idea, and he agreed.

Art went over to the house to check it out, and when he came back, we talked about the ideas I had and laid out a plan. Art and I decided to go into it together, so we signed a contract, and I immediately began planning the interior design work for Singing Pines. I was doing what I loved again and everything seemed to be working out perfectly.

According to Art, "Dorris was ecstatic. She was hustling around, saying how this room would be this, the other room would be that."

When we finally had a feasible plan that included six bedrooms, it was time to really dive into the project.

"Okay," I told Art one day, "now it's time to do it."

I hired some painters and paperhangers, and was once again coordinating a big project. It was tiring, but it was wonderful.

"Dorris is a slave-driver," Art said with a laugh. "I was shanghaied for six days nonstop — from dawn until two in the morning — and put to work putting beds together, attaching mirrors to the bureaus, fixing showers, hanging art on walls. It about drove me crazy, but I couldn't complain because Dorris was working right along with me at that same pace."

I had already sent out flyers announcing the opening date, so we were in a bit of a rush.

"It was a crash program," Art agrees. "People were booked up, so we had to finish. No ifs, ands or buts."

And we finished. The landscapers were just leaving just as the first guests were arriving, but we did it, and it was beautiful.

We kept Singing Pines open for two years, and I thoroughly enjoyed every minute of it. Even though I had never been much in the kitchen, I did all of the cooking, and I got to be pretty good at it. I had returned to a busy life and, once again, I started feeling like there were never enough hours in the day to do it all.

As much as I loved Singing Pines, and as much as I wanted to keep it forever, we had to close it in 1993. We simply couldn't make enough money to pay the mortgage and it just didn't make sense to keep it open anymore.

In 1994, Betty told me about Charlotte, a wealthy woman who wanted someone to cook for her and keep her company for a couple of months. Ever since I'd been in rehabilitation, I had been feeling like I wanted to be helping people more, and so I agreed to go have lunch with her and talk about this opportunity.

Charlotte's gorgeous glass house, situated on a large lake, shocked and astounded me. I wouldn't even begin to guess how much it was worth, but she was worth millions. After a very elaborate lunch with this gentlewoman, she explained that she'd pay me well if I would see after her and make sure she had the right kind of food on the table. I didn't see anything wrong with that, so I signed the contract and started the following week.

I stayed in the swankiest bedroom I'd ever seen and I had a huge bathroom with a Jacuzzi in it. There was another, more lavish Jacuzzi downstairs that hadn't been used for ten years. Charlotte wanted me to get in the downstairs Jacuzzi two or three times a day because she thought it would be good for me and she had arranged it all.

I didn't feel as if I was working for her at all; she treated me like a queen. The only thing I really did for her was bake fresh biscuits every morning and fresh cornbread every day. She even gave me a brand-new Cadillac with gold-plated locks to drive. I was using only a cane at this point, and I hadn't done much driving at all. She explained by saying she wanted people to be impressed with me.

Charlotte gave me two days off every week and I'd take the car, get my friends and go shopping. I usually had them drive, though, just because I wasn't comfortable with it yet. My friends benefited from the job almost as much as I did — with the exception of the pay. I called them to come over with their bathing suits so they could go in the Jacuzzi with me.

One day, Betty Micheli came over and she got a wild hair. "Let's go skinny dipping."

"No," I said, a little shocked. "Somebody will see us."

"Nobody can see us."

"We're sitting here with glass walls around us," I said, "and there are boats running up and down the lake. They're liable to look in."

"Come on," she prodded. "They can't see us."

Finally, she talked me into it and just as soon as we took off our clothes and jumped into the Jacuzzi in the sunroom, the groundskeeper came sauntering in.

"Dorris, what are you doing?" he asked. I'm still not sure if he could see us.

"Don't come in here," I said. So frightened he was going to see us, I panicked. And of course he wanted to know why we didn't want him to come any farther inside. "Just don't come in. Come back later!"

Betty thought it was hilarious, but I was pretty shaken by the whole thing.

My experiences at that house were all pretty wild. I was only there for two and a half months, but it included the holiday season, which was somewhat strange. Charlotte had never once had a Christmas tree!

When I suggested that she get a tree before Christmas had come and gone, she looked at me and said, "Dorris, honey, I've never had a Christmas tree in this house."

"Well," I said, "I'm here now and we're going to have a Christmas tree."

Charlotte agreed to give me money for a tree and ornaments. I talked to one of the groundskeepers, who agreed to go with me to get a tree. We took his Buick over to the Christmas tree farm and, after inspecting each one, we picked out the very biggest tree and hauled it back to her house. The poor woman didn't know what to do. The tree spread across half of the living room and she just kind of gaped at it while I handed the tinsel and ornaments to the yardman while he stood on the ladder and decorated the tree. Using an angel theme, it turned out beautifully. She loved it; I think my decorating skill impressed her.

Living there was definitely an experience, but I never felt I was really helping Charlotte out. I didn't feel I was accomplishing anything and, even though I was making a lot of money, I felt I was wasting my time. I wanted to work for someone who needed me, not someone who simply wanted someone to help her entertain and dress up. It was a short-term job anyway, but I actually quit a little bit early. I just couldn't be satisfied doing something that didn't benefit someone or something in the end.

"Dorris was determined to work for something," Art said.

"That was part of her recovery. I've seen plenty of people who went from feeling down to getting back up again, even when all the odds were stacked against them. Dorris was always telling the world, 'Yes I can, and I will prove to you that I can.'

"Everybody who sold her short, she proved wrong. My experience is that people like Dorris who push everybody to do their best are the people that do the best. That is the absolute critical factor, the bottom line. The road to recovery, from a rehabilitation standpoint, requires determination and confidence that you can and will make it. You have to push the people working with you. That way you're making sure that everything possible is being done, and then anything is possible."

The next year I got an intriguing phone call from Art. His mother owned an old Advance Auto Parts building that his father had bought in Covington, Virginia, that had recently become vacant. He wanted to do something with it, and he was thinking of opening a craft store, since crafts are big in Covington.

"My mother wanted me to open an antique shop," Art explains, "but I told her I didn't think an antique shop in downtown Covington would really go. I started talking to some friends, and many people told me that there are a lot of crafters in Covington, and that's how the idea got started."

Art took a trip to Lexington and then to Roanoke to look at other craft stores, and he decided that that was what he wanted to do.

"I called Dorris to tell her about my idea," Art remembers. "I told her about the craft shops and how I thought she might be interested in designing the store for me."

I was open to anything at that point and said I'd help Art out. He wanted to show me the building, and he also wanted to stop in Roanoke so I could visualize what he was talking about. So we took a little trip to Virginia and, when we returned to Covington, we met with a contractor.

The building was completely gutted, which reminded me of

the big hotels I used to do. Just walking through the place got me excited about renovating again. That whole feeling of accomplishment came over me in a wave, and I got really enthusiastic about the project.

We sat down to plan the design of the shop and the project was soon underway. The outside was designed with a colonial look and the inside with a formal garden theme. I wanted people to walk into the wicker area and visualize a garden and then go into the elegant and delicate formal dining room with Queen Anne style furniture. It was definitely a challenge, but it did prove that any building can be brightened up with the right touch.

I told Art which colors of paint to buy, and he kept the workers filled in on what they were supposed to be doing. But if there's one thing I've learned, it's that if you want something done right, you better do it yourself. I'd always lived by that policy before, and should have stuck to it, but I made sure never to forget that rule ever again.

"It was right at the end of the renovating, and we ended up with another crash program," Art says, shaking his head. "I had three painters and all the paint, ready to go. But, as it turned out, I had bought too much of one paint and too little of another. I'd changed the colors completely! So I told the painter which paint goes where, and the painter said he didn't think so.

"I said, 'That's what Dorris said.' But I had misunderstood. When Dorris came in the week before the Grand Opening, she screamed."

It was bright green paint, and was completely wrong. I had to change the color at the last minute and the poor painters had to paint day and night for three days in order finish. On the last night, the carpenter was there until two in the morning. He even got his wife come in for the whole last week — and she was a doctor. Somehow, however, we finished before the next morning and the Grand Opening party was a real celebration.

"Dorris was amazing," Art says. "She didn't have all the

people working for her, and she couldn't climb the ladders or put borders in like she used to, but she still had the talent and she could still use it. She changed her vision. She wasn't able to do the high wire walking that she used to do, but she still had that eye for making things look elegant. It really was gorgeous. And she proved that she could do whatever she wanted to do."

Art is right; I had proved that I could do what I wanted to do, but I hadn't done that alone. It was my belief in myself and my faith in God that led me to the place I wanted to be. The doctors at Fort Sanders Regional Hospital had said I would never walk again and I had taken that as a personal challenge. It was a challenge that I met with lots of hard work, a positive attitude, and an unfaltering faith in God.

In order to carry my faith out and actualize my love for God, I had joined Trinity Broadcasting System and become a partner of the Rev. Benny Hinn, a television evangelist. Although I had walked with my walker before, the first time I actually walked by myself since I'd come down with GBS was when I went to a Benny Hinn healing service. The singing lifted my soul and when prayers began, I was walking! I took about ten or fifteen steps all by myself. But I knew I hadn't really done it all by myself; I knew God had a big part in it.

I was walking, I was well, I was a survivor and I wanted to make a new life for myself that showed my gratitude for God's grace. I began attending a lot of crusades, and the singing spoke to my soul. But that was just a feeling I had. I didn't know just how good those crusades were until one stormy night in Memphis.

It was the second night of the crusade and the services had been wonderful and peaceful, but just as the service was ending that second night, I could hear the wind howling outside. I knew that there was a big storm coming.

When my helper and I were ready to leave, I pushed the door open. The wind caught me and I was tossed down fifteen concrete steps. I pulled my helper down with me, and though she fell too, they thought I had a broken neck and a broken back.

Someone called an ambulance. When the paramedics came, they put me on a back board, since they were almost positive I had damaged my spinal cord. Benny Hinn's wife, Suzanne, showed up within minutes after I'd arrived in the emergency room.

"Can we pray that no bones were broken?" she asked the doctor.

"I don't believe in you holy-roller people," he said.

"It's me they're praying for, not you, Doctor," I told him.

"If you could only see yourself," he said. "You're neck is surely broken, and your back. . . . Look at her."

"Jesus sees her," someone with Suzanne said.

"I don't believe in this!" he said, but he walked away and let them pray.

They laid hands on my neck and my back and asked God that no bones would be broken. As they did it, I felt a great warmth wrap my body like an electric blanket.

"Lord, touch her body. We can handle bruises and scratches, but we don't want her bones to be broken."

The doctor was right about one thing: I looked horrible. I looked like someone had chewed me up and spit me out. My glasses were broken, the skin on my cheeks had been scraped away, my nose was bruised, and my mouth was bleeding.

But the doctor had been wrong about the most important thing: I didn't have any broken bones. He hadn't believed.

Chapter Seven:
God's Recovery Toolkit:
Belief, Initiative, and Action

FAITH IN GOD'S HEALING POWER can be a force in your life that brings you exactly what you need. That's what happened for me; it can happen for you. The course of action I took in my recovery process was based on my faith.

This is not to say that I had faith in my actions; on the contrary, I knew that I was powerless on my own. But I also knew that God would help me if I helped myself. And that combination worked! What I believed plus how I acted on my beliefs healed my body.

I went from a paralyzed, helpless invalid of Guillain Barré Syndrome — one who needed to be totally cared for — to a strong, helpful caregiver. I spent two full years of my life holding onto my beliefs, remaining positive, demanding the most out of myself and out of my doctors, and abiding by my faith.

I now spend my time teaching patients of debilitating diseases such as Guillain Barré how to overcome their illnesses. I remind them that yes, it is hard to pull yourself through the bad times, but each new day is going to be more beautiful than the one before. With a positive attitude, unfaltering determination, and constant faith, you will reach your highest potential. You have to remember that your life matters and you must be willing to fight for it.

According to Dr. Blake, "Spirit is very, very important in a patient's recovery. In general, people who keep a positive attitude just do better. The patients who tell themselves, 'I'm going to get better. I'm going to work hard and get through this thing, however long it takes,' tend to do just that."

I understand that maintaining a positive attitude is not easy for ill people to whom such an outlook doesn't come naturally. Indeed, it is easy to get wrapped up in self-pity and despair, but taking an active role in the recovery process can make all the difference.

Families and friends should also be active in the patient's care, which can help him from feeling isolated and lonely and ultimately save his overall attitude. Although most patients' attitudes will change dramatically by being kept informed, it is important that the expression of negative emotional reactions never be discouraged. For many people, simply voicing the angers and fears they have is enough to relieve them. Even if it means the occasional outburst, everything within the doctors' control should be done to foster an overall good attitude for the patient.

BELIEF

Belief that you will recover is a critical component of the toolkit. It is not, however, all you need to be able to restore your health; you must act on your beliefs. Likewise, there are many people who are industrious without belief. They act out of fear and desperation; they are wishful, but hopeless. For the best possible results to occur, both sides of this equation are necessary. Belief on its own is never enough and neither is action.

The underlying principle of this toolkit is this: What you believe and how you act on your beliefs makes the difference between sickness and health. All the strategies that I used were based on these principles. During my ordeal with GBS, I found continuous validation every day in the old saying, "God helps those who help themselves."

I have always believed that God has a purpose in my life, signifying that my recovery was momentous; I had to recover in order to continue carrying out my purpose. I had always thought that my purpose was to make people happy through improving and beautifying their environment. As I recovered, however, I began to realize just how important my recovery was; God wanted me to help others recover, too.

Having a deep and compelling belief provides the fuel to move forward and achieve results. I admit, it is hard to really believe — to be so sure of yourself and your abilities that nothing can change your mind — but what you must remember is that belief is the driving force behind any abilities you have. Belief is your anchoring force and without it, you can easily stray from your goals. Remember to set new, attainable goals everyday. The more you reach, the more belief you have in yourself, the more confidence you build in your abilities.

INITIATIVE

Initiative is also a major recovery tool. In my case, it resulted in learning about my own disease and pushing my doctors and my therapists to do everything within their power to make my belief in my recovery a reality.

From that first interview in Intensive Care to my demanding to use the exercise bicycle as an outpatient in the Patricia Neal Rehabilitation Center, I pushed my caregivers to push me. There's no doubt about it: I was a nuisance to my doctors. But without the demands I put upon them, I wouldn't have gotten as far as I did, or as fast. I wasn't just being a needy complainer; I was urging everyone to do their best.

Sometimes, as when we are in miserable and seemingly hopeless situations, it is easier to believe in anything other than ourselves. For these times, focus your belief in God. Know that He will not let you fail at attaining your goals and that He will take care of you. One Guillain Barré Syndrome sufferer that I talked to recently told me that she wouldn't have made it to the rehabilitation stage of the disease if she hadn't known that God would see her through. She has been walking on her own for three months now, and she is sure that it was her belief that allowed her to do that.

"I remember when I couldn't even move the muscles in my face, and I remember my husband crying next to my hospital bed," she said. "I couldn't talk, but I could write just a little bit, so I took my pen and paper and I asked him why he was crying.

"'I'm going to miss your smile,' he said.

"'God will take care of that,' I wrote. And He did. I can smile again. I can't frown, but who wants to frown, anyway? To believe that God will see you through is to believe in yourself. That's what I've learned throughout this whole ordeal."

ACTION

Without action, your belief cannot do much for you at all. I didn't just sit around trying to convince myself that I was going to get through this — I acted! This is always a challenge, and even more so when you are paralyzed. But I struggled to use and expand every bit of mobility I had.

And I kept my mind active. Unlike some GBS patients, I could still talk, so I was able to reach out to others. But even those who are unable to talk can act on their beliefs, and one of the most important actions one can take is developing a positive attitude. It is important to try to work with what you have. If one leg is cut off, see what you can do with the other leg. If you can learn to think in those terms and figure out what you can do to change things, you can foster some hope in yourself, and with hope comes recovery.

I was talking to a GBS survivor not long ago, and I was fascinated by his attitude. Even though his hands were paralyzed and even though he was on a ventilator, unable to communicate, he was able to maintain a positive outlook. Luckily, I retained my ability to talk, but according to this patient, I missed out!

"It was actually kind of interesting," he told me later. "You don't realize what kind of stupid things you say when you're engaging in conversation, but once you're unable to be a part of a discussion, you begin listening to what people are saying and you start thinking how ridiculous they sound. I spent a lot of time laughing to myself. Sometimes I would think out replies to the doctors' comments, and they were usually pretty wry and smart-alecky because people don't hear the literal implications of what they're saying most of the time.

"I remember when the doctor told me I could talk again, and I felt like the game was over," he went on. "I was relieved, but it was kind of like, 'Well, that's one perspective I'll never have again.' But, of course, I was delighted to be able to talk again and, once I'd readjusted to the whole sensation of having words come out of my mouth, I don't think I shut up for days! I talked myself hoarse in no time and one of the nurses said I was a lot more compliant when I couldn't talk. If only she'd known what I was thinking that whole time!"

So, a positive attitude can be maintained no matter how serious the patient's condition. It is, of course, much easier to be positive when things are going well. In fact, when you're suffering, it often seems so much easier to give up.

It's true: things can get scary at the beginning. Finding yourself suddenly unable to move is definitely disturbing. You are utterly helpless, and in light of the doctors' uncertainty about GBS, it is easy to feel hopeless. Since there is little that they can predict about recovery, most doctors give an array of possibilities, from 100 percent recovery to permanent disability and even death.

Emotional reactions to the unpredictability of their outcome are extremely varied, and I know of many patients who became depressed and discouraged when they were first diagnosed with GBS. Most patients get better, however, and are eventually able to function normally. Doctors can often be catalysts for the feelings of hopelessness, but as a little research shows, as I said before, there is hope. And the more confidence a patient has in his recovery, the more likely he is to recover.

Oftentimes, as in my case, doctors tell patients the worst-case scenarios. One patient I met, who is now walking with a cane, was in very critical condition. She had gone into a coma and the doctors met with her family to tell them there was no hope. They even told her family to make funeral arrangements. Before long, however, she was on the road to recovery. This woman attributes her recovery to God's grace, and I would have to agree with her there.

Too many doctors simply do not motivate their patients enough, which is unfortunate because motivation is a crucial element in developing a positive attitude. Some doctors give "gloom and doom" when they're telling you about your condition — the last thing patients need to hear. Especially in the early stages of a disease, it is important that medical personnel talk about the bright side of things. How can you be expected to have a positive attitude when you're thinking about dark, harsh, depressing things instead of the beautiful things in the world like the sun and fragrant flowers?

People don't need to hear about all the horrible things that are going to happen to them at the beginning of any disease. They need to know all the possibilities of recovery, and all the positive things that the doctors can do for them. For those whose doctors bombard their patients with negative news at the onset of the condition, I strongly urge that this information be saved for later and that positive elements should first be emphasized, such as the high recovery rate of GBS.

Patients should inform their doctors of the need for incentive to motivate the process of rapid improvement. The depressing outlook often offered at the outset is not at all helpful. If the doctor is unable to give a brighter outlook, another doctor, one who can better motivate recovery, is necessary.

One patient said that if it had not been for the confidence that his family gave him, he would have given up. "The doctors kept telling me all these negative things and I was devastated," he said. "I was ready to die. Then one day my uncle came into my room, and said, 'Guess what? I've been at the library all day, and everything I read says that Guillain Barré Syndrome is not permanent. You're going to get past this!'

"It wasn't until that moment that I started fighting GBS, and that's what you've got to do: fight it with everything you have. First you have to accept it, then you have to fight it. There are many horrible things you can start thinking while you're lying in that bed, and the only thing I can say about that is to be patient, be smart, and be glad you're still alive."

Just the other day, somebody told me that survival takes character, and I think they are right. And I'm convinced that everyone has character; they just have to know when to apply it. For anyone who isn't sure, the answer is NOW!

Use your personality's most endearing quality to overcome the obstacles that you face, because often it's that strong point in your character that can pull you through.

We are all different, and we all have different ways of handling negative situations, but nine times out of ten the way we handle such situations is the best way for us individually. Use whatever strength you can muster and focus it on your recovery. Your survival is one of those conditions for which "Whatever works!" applies.

The way people react to their conditions in the very beginning is often the deciding factor in how they will react to it in the end. When I first became ill, I reacted the way most people do: I didn't believe it. I denied that this could really be happening to me and I was sure that I had something more common and more short-lived than GBS. It was a shock to accept the seriousness of my condition and reconcile myself to a lengthy recovery period. But frankly, I never accepted that it could get the better of me, and I think that my refusal to be the victim of the condition was beneficial in my recovery.

Another common reaction that I had, and that probably ended up aiding me in the long run, was pure frustration. I didn't want to be in the hospital, and it annoyed me that I had to depend on other people. My exasperation with my situation was a major incentive in my determination to recover as soon as possible.

One patient recalls the first time he got out of bed after two months, and how the nurse's reaction to his fear made him never want to try it again. "I think I made a little whimpering noise or something," he recalled, "which is understandable, considering it looked like the floor was about a mile away from me and I felt like my feet were detached from my body.

"The nurse told me, and I quote, to 'be quiet and hurry up.' I just looked at her and told her to put me back in bed. It's not like I'd had a bad attitude the entire time, I just didn't want to be criticized for being a little nervous about trying something so momentous."

The emotions that accompany conditions like Guillain Barré Syndrome can be very disturbing and are always very real. It is important that they be given the attention that they deserve rather than be brushed off as irrational or silly.

It is not at all abnormal for Guillain Barré Syndrome patients to suffer from panic attacks, especially when the illness has affected their breathing. However, it's not just when a patient is first unable to breathe that this sense of panic occurs; in fact, it is very common for patients to reach this point when they are first taken off their respirators. Doctors and nurses often have a hard time empathizing with patients since they recognize that they are actually getting better. Nevertheless, it is important for them to realize that the patient has been dependent on a machine for some time and it is very scary to suddenly be told that it's time for him to take over and do it on his own.

Although I was fortunate enough not to have to deal with it, I have been told that it feels something like being "ripped away from the womb." One patient told me that she had formed an emotional attachment to her respirator and when they took her off of it she was sure she was going to die.

Doctors can also ensure that their patients are able to have the best possible outlook by preventing them from taking certain drugs. At least one drug given to GBS patients actually causes depression. Patients should be sure to ask what the side effects of all drugs are before they take them. If depression is one of the side effects, ask whether or not there is any other drug that can be used to treat the same condition that does not have this side effect.

Maintaining a positive attitude is something that is important from the beginning to the end. It is crucial in the beginning since it is at this point that the patient needs to be motivated to overcome the disease, but it is just as crucial as the patient is recovering. Many patients find it difficult to move from the hospital to the rehabilitation center.

"I felt like I was being torn away from the people who understood me," one patient relayed to me. "I began feeling sorry for myself and I thought that my therapists were out to get me."

The transition can be eased by visits from the future therapists while the patient is still in the hospital. Likewise, it is helpful for the patients' doctors to visit the patient in rehab. Great measure should be taken to make this transition comfortable; rehabilitation is one of the most important parts of recovery.

"I have worked as a rehabilitation counselor for twelve years," Darryl Monday of the Patricia Neal Rehabilitation Center said. "I've evaluated over 400 people and trained several hundred, and the one common denominator — and every rehabilitation counselor will tell you this — is if the patient has determination and a positive attitude, if they put the maximum into it, not the minimum, that's when you get results.

"I'm always delighted with people like Dorris. You want them to succeed. I think that Dorris is at the point she is today because she wanted to be there. She forced herself to be there. Dorris never gave up. And I think that is the whole fact, really, in a nutshell; you can make it if you don't give up. The thing that strikes me about her is that, from day one, she has had one of the most positive and determined attitudes of anyone I've ever talked to."

What's important to keep in mind, however, is that anyone can create a positive attitude for themselves. A major factor in promoting a positive attitude in yourself comes with remaining active in your treatment and in your recovery. Instead of passively allowing the doctors to take charge, *you* take charge. After all, it is your body. The more control you take, the more your outlook will improve.

Demanding the most from yourself and from your caregivers is another factor in the action element of this recovery formula. By acting on your belief, you will be demanding more out of yourself. And, as you've probably noticed, I was very demanding from the beginning to the end. I believed that I could overcome this disease, and I made sure that everything I could possibly do to reach that goal was being done.

I found out later that "problem patients" often have better recovery rates. It makes sense. The "good" patients give up personal responsibility for their recovery; they cooperate with the experts and assume that the doctors know best. But no one knows my body as well as I do. Sure, doctors know the names for things and have medical skills that I don't have. I knew they were equipped to help me, but I also knew I had to help myself. That meant pestering them to do their best for me and to respond specifically to my special needs. Guillain Barré Syndrome is a very individualized disease and doctors must remember that there is no "average" when it comes to this condition.

Not only will demanding the most out of your caregivers provide a whole new realm of possibilities in your recovery, but it will also provide you with a feeling of control and, thus, a positive attitude.

"My decision to focus on getting better and my insisting that the doctors do everything possible improved my attitude and strengthened my ability to recover," said one GBS survivor who made a ninety percent recovery. "Without my positive outlook, I would never have improved as much I did."

Not only does feeding your body the proper fuel improve your physical wellbeing, but it also helps foster the attitude that is so important in recovery! For this reason, I cannot stress enough the importance of finding a nutritional program that allows your body to be its best. The results I had are not abnormal; nutritional supplementation consistently improves overall well-being.

I suggest that everyone get on a nutritional program, whether sick or not. It is something from which everyone can benefit. I will never stop taking the supplements because I know I feel more alive now than I've ever felt before.

"The moral of the story," said Dr. Winfred Holt, "is that no matter what you are confronted with, no matter how tragic or traumatic, you can be a survivor."

You cannot, however, be a true survivor until you have used what you've learned to help someone else. You can't fully recover if you stop working once you're doing better; you have to share what you've learned about the recovery, yourself, and God with others.

No matter how good your attitude is, no matter how demanding you were on yourself and your caregivers, and no matter how much respect you gave your body, your belief can never be substantial if you do not carry out this duty. Without this step you might as well have walked a thousand miles through the desert for no other purpose than to have done it. Not only to help others and reward yourself, but also to thank God for His support, act on your beliefs.

When I began to help other patients at the Patricia Neal Rehabilitation Center, it was not just because my doctors thought my attitude and inspiring example could help depressed patients overcome their perception of being permanently handicapped. I had already considered using my knowledge of recovery and the essential components of it to help victims of debilitating diseases. It occurred to me when I was at Fort Sanders Regional Hospital that I decided that I wanted to help patients foster a positive attitude in themselves. It wasn't until I was at Patricia Neal, however, that I made a conscious decision to help others in this way.

Once an outpatient, I became more aware of disabled people and their special needs, and I began to realize that there are a lot of ways that life could be made a little easier for them. I gained a personal understanding of what it was like for people in wheelchairs and people with canes or walkers. Because I understood what it is like to be disabled and was fortunate enough to recover from that state, I knew I had an important responsibility: help make life a little easier for as many handicapped people as I could.

I never stopped seeing patients from the Patricia Neal Rehabilitation Center, and though my experience with the wealthy woman had been a flop, it became my goal to become a full-time caregiver. Until I found that position, however, I was happy talking to patients from the Rehab Center who needed a little uplifting. Doctors from all over the region referred any Guillain Barré Syndrome patients to me, and I was always happy to share what I'd learned and offer a little encouragement.

"Dorris is really good at pep talks," Betty said. "She shares her story, encourages people when they are down and gives them a little jump-start."

I get a lot of phone calls from GBS patients around the area saying, "I'm dead, I'm dead, I can't do anything."

They tell me everything that's going wrong, and I say to them, "You're here today, you have a future, and you can do something with your future. Look what I've done."

I try to motivate people to look ahead and see that their future is bright. If they can see that, then they're more willing to maximize their potential by doing everything they can to recover as soon as possible.

"Remember your goal," I tell them. "Your immediate goal can't be to recover every detail of your past. You have to create a future for yourself first; then you can face the various challenges. One step at a time."

As far as I'd come, I knew I was never going to be the same as I'd been before GBS had struck. I wouldn't, for example, be going out to dance as much. I've gone dancing twice, but it was difficult. I get tired much sooner than I used to. There are a lot of things that burn me out quickly, like my annual trip to Athens, Tennessee, with my family. We used to go out there and stay with our friends overnight, but now I get too worn out to stay all night. But still, I get out and do things. I do as much as my body will let me.

"Dorris," a GBS patient said to me the other day, "I just don't understand you. You just flit around everywhere."

"Well," I said, "I make myself do things. A lot of times I don't sit down, I don't lie down, I just keep going."

"Not me," he said. "My paralysis gets worse and worse, and the more time passes, the more handicapped I get."

"You're not making yourself move," I told him. "The more you sit, the easier it is to sit and the harder it is to stand. If you're going to get better, you've got to believe that you're going to get better and you've got to demand yourself to get better. It wasn't easy for me to climb stairs and take showers when I was in my wheelchair, but I made myself do it, because I knew I could. That's how you get better."

He just shook his head and stared at me like he couldn't believe a word I was saying. "Dorris," he said after a few seconds, "why don't you start an organization. Do you know how many

GBS victims there are in east Tennessee alone?"

"You just made your first mistake right there," I said, ignoring his question. "You identified yourself as a victim. Start identifying yourself as a survivor because if you believe you're a victim, that's all you'll ever be."

Fostering the right attitude is the hardest thing a caregiver can do, because people who are determined that they're in a bad situation truly are in a bad situation. The patients able to see past their temporary grief and into the future, however, are inspirational.

Most patients let go of their discouragement as soon as they've made some kind of progress — no matter how small. The problem with GBS, of course, is that patients usually get worse before they get better. Once they are comfortable with their surroundings and with their situation, however, most patients can see the brighter side of things.

There were a few Guillain Barré Syndrome patients at Fort Sanders Regional Medical Center or at Patricia Neal, and I was sure to talk to them. It was always an inspiring feeling for me to watch them as they progressed through their recovery. I remember one GBS patient at Patricia Neal who fought every day for weeks to strengthen her muscles. Every time I went to see her, she would describe her accomplishments since our last visit. "I can change channels on the TV," she said with enormous pride one day.

Another day, when I just happened to be in the dining hall of the Center, I watched as she pushed herself out of her wheelchair and walked over to her table on her own two feet. I started clapping immediately and the rest of the patients soon joined in. She looked up at me and smiled, and I knew exactly how she felt. It was one of the happiest moments in her life.

Every sufferer of a debilitating disease deserves the chance to have that kind of moment, and it's what I wanted to help them achieve. In 1994, I finally got the chance to give my full attention to somebody who needed daily motivation and support. I began working for Luke Bowman, as a caregiver for his mother Jean, who had Alzheimer's disease. Luke badly needed someone to watch out for her and make sure that she took her medicine and did her exercises. I lived with them and took care of Jean for two and a half years while helping Art with his craft store in Virginia.

"At first Jean Bowman wouldn't get out of her chair," my good friend Betty recalled. "She just moped around all the time. But, of course, once Dorris came into the picture, things changed. Dorris won't stand for moping! She got Jean interested in the things around her, took her shopping and out to eat. Dorris even brought her to a couple of Christmas parties that year! She really helped her climb out of her shell."

Jean had built a wall around herself and I spent a year and a half deconstructing it. As is usually the case, her own children couldn't get through to her. It is usually someone without any kind of attachments who is able to get through to patients in her condition. But seeing her taking an interest in life was a reward both for me and her family.

Being a full-time caregiver for a seriously debilitated patient isn't easy, but it is very rewarding. It is important to put yourself in the patient's place and to be very understanding and loving. To give love is to be loved. The rest will follow.

Helping others face the challenges that you have met, even if you are not cut out for being a full-time caretaker, is vital and advantageous. Talk to people, listen to their problems and help them through the tough times. There is no reward like knowing you've made a difference in someone's life.

Helping others is a fundamental part of one's own recovery, and it is one of the most satisfying components. I did not wait until I was healed to begin trying to help other patients, and I think that was one of the major reasons that I recovered as quickly as I did. Just knowing that you are giving of yourself during a time that selfishness is acceptable can foster belief in yourself.

The ability to make someone else a little better is far more rewarding than the ability to make yourself better. It is easy to excuse ourselves from helping others, especially if we are dealing with serious personal problems, but self-centeredness is a disease in and of itself. An important part of recovery is to regain the lost sense of responsibility for others. This is how God acts through people and it's how we prove our love for Him.

Belief, then, is acted upon through a positive attitude, a demand for the most from oneself and from one's caretakers, a respect for one's body and a generous willingness to help others. If one is able to act on his belief in such ways, then he has almost attained the goal of this recovery toolkit: faith.

Through acting on your beliefs, you will master faith, the only true ingredient in recovery, really the only ingredient in my recovery plan. Without the action you can only have belief, and without the belief, you can never achieve faith. Once you've acted on your belief, then you have affirmed your faith. They go hand in hand; acting on your belief in yourself and your own abilities and doing everything to prove it means having faith, and having faith means accepting your responsibility to help yourself so that you can help and teach others.

Chapter Eight:
Repaying the Gift

N O MATTER OUR CONDITION, we can still improve ourselves. Every day I wake up looking forward to doing it. To be everything we can possibly be and do everything we can possibly do is an exciting prospect. If we take that prospect step by step — meeting hourly and daily goals — we can ensure ourselves a meaningful and estimable life.

If, however, exterior circumstances prevent us from meeting our goals, we must adjust to the situation, revise our goals and continue to reach for our highest potential. Nothing can stop us from being our best, and nothing can keep us from making our lives substantial and worthwhile. Life is an extremely exhilarating endeavor — something to be cherished — and just knowing you can always make it better than it already is incredibly uplifting.

What's so wonderful is that, not only are we here to make the best of the time we have, but we are also offered numerous opportunities to help other people better their lives. Think about the hundreds of people you encounter each and every day. By recognizing each encounter as an opportunity to help others, a staggering amount of improvement could result from your efforts.

Often, ensuring that everything possible is being done to aid your recovery means exploring new possibilities. In my case, that included natural nutritional supplements. It's discouraging how little medical doctors know about nutrition; they are taught almost nothing about it in medical school. It's hard to believe that this important subject gets largely ignored. Most of us, myself included, have to get seriously ill before we pay attention to the proper feeding of our bodies. It surprises me how few people investigate what they put into their bodies. However, it didn't surprise or even dawn on me until I met Winferd Holt, D.D.S., a dentist-turned-nutritionist, who gave a public lecture on nutrition which I attended.

"It was a seminar focusing on the importance of nutritional supplementation," Dr. Holt said. "I used this crude scenario: if you drive a standard automobile, you fill it with gasoline, not diesel. It won't run on the wrong fuel. We care about the quality of gas and oil for our cars, for we understand that it makes a difference to how well our cars will run. Still, we don't take the same attitude with our own bodies. In fact, few of us even think about supplying our bodies with the proper nutrients."

Everything Dr. Holt said that night made perfect sense to me, and the more I listened to him, the more I realized how deficient in all the essential nourishment my body must have been. Although I've always been conscious of what I eat – limiting junk food and fatty foods – I'd never really considered all the basic minerals and vitamins that my body needs in order to thrive.

"What most of us do not realize," Dr. Holt said, "is that during this day and age, our bodies are more deprived of vital nutrients than they have ever been before. The main reason for that is the depletion of nutrients in our soil, which results from our agricultural practices – using insecticides and pesticides on plants and using antibiotics and hormones on animals. As a result, our bodies are bombarded by all these things that literally lower our resistance. With a lowered immune system, the effects of disease are magnified. When you strengthen the immune system, however, your body can withstand more and recover more quickly.

"Another reason for our society's lowered immune system," Dr. Holt continued, "is our excessive use of antibiotics. When antibiotics came onto the scene, everyone thought that by taking this pill we could combat almost anything. Now, however, we know that our bodies build up resistance to these drugs, therefore lowering our immune systems, and that our bodies have so many anti-drug reactions, such as the lowered immune system, that we are unable to resist disease. The body breaks down gradually. Disease doesn't happen overnight."

I was, at that point, walking with a cane and suffering from tremors and a lack of energy. I was no longer being attacked by Guillain Barré Syndrome, but I was still dealing with the aftermath and hadn't reached my potential. After listening to just a few minutes of Dr. Holt's lecture, I had no doubt that, even though I was not currently suffering from any disease, my body would benefit from nutritional supplements.

"Each of us is our own best doctor," Dr. Holt said. "It is your responsibility to protect your own health. To reach optimal health, you have to make sure that your body is provided with every nutrient that we know about. Nutrition has always been around, but hasn't been in vogue until the last few years. If we get our immune systems strong enough, then we can resist not only the common bugs, but also many of these diseases that are now plaguing our society."

While many recovering GBS patients think they are past their disease and are done with recovery despite their various residual effects, I knew that there were still ways to improve my condition. I also believed that there must be treatments beyond medication and physical therapy, which were the two main methods by which I'd been treated up to that point. Until that night, however, I was unaware of what more I could do.

"That night I was discussing the benefits of natural supplements and how our bodies respond to nutritional support," says Dr. Holt. "I told people in the group about the basic things necessary for the body to maintain its health; the body needs a balanced nutritional regime, not just a pill here or there."

What attracted me to the idea of a nutritional program was the fact that they're not only for people who are suffering from an illness, but they're also for anyone else who cares about his body. I'd come to realize that night that, though I'd thought I was giving my body the best possible care, I was falling short in quite a few areas.

"Nutrition isn't a treatment for symptoms and diseases," Dr. Holt emphasized. "It's about making sure the body gets what it needs."

That said, I grew excited about the program and the more I listened, the more fascinated I became.

"I introduced to the group the program that my wife and I use," Dr. Holt says. "I recommend it to anyone. My dental patients who follow the plan see remarkable results. I've never found anything that compares to the application of proper nutritional support. The end results are amazing. Whether my patients' gums are bleeding, infected, or losing bone, when I give them what their bodies need, the recovery is faster and the diseases don't come back."

The first step, Dr. Holt said, is to clean out the colon because if it isn't working, the toxins are reabsorbed. He then described the various enzymes, proteins, nucleic acids, amino acids, and herbs that can accomplish this. But it was the success story of a complete vitamin with minerals and trace minerals that really compelled me.

"I was introduced to this supplement by a physician at Johns Hopkins University," Dr. Holt told us. "He had a private practice and, at fifty years of age, he had a heart disease. He was told that he only had five months to live, and that's when he started himself on a nutritional program which included all of the seventytwo trace minerals. He survived to eighty-nine years of age and, until the day he died, he used his nutritional approach in his medical practice."

Beating the odds — that's what I wanted to do. So, as soon as Dr. Holt's seminar had ended, I made my way up to the front of the room to tell him my story and to see what he suggested.

"When she told me her story, I felt she was fortunate to have recovered as much as she had from Guillain Barré Syndrome," Dr. Holt said. "I noticed right away that she was very shaky, and she told me that she still had tremors and that she had very little energy. She had already fought a courageous battle and still, she was seeking anything that would assist her further."

Sometimes my shaking would seriously hinder my ability to stand, usually when I was very tired. I told him how I had been to many doctors, and how they'd all told me that I'd have to live with this the best I could. Many recovering GBS patients listen to their doctors and believe that they have done everything that is possible in order to recover and that they are not going to get any better. My doctors had told me this time and time again, but I stuck to my belief and was ready to act on it.

"I don't believe them," I said. "I believe in myself, and I'm willing to do whatever it takes to recover some more. I know it's possible and I think a nutritional program could help me."

Dr. Holt sat down with me and we talked about the best supportive approach for my condition. I was thrilled to be finally taking a new course of action, and I was convinced that the supplements were going to be a great asset.

"I started Dorris on a basic, broad spectrum approach that incorporated enzymes, minerals, vitamins, herbs, and fiber," Dr. Holt says. "That's the basic support your body needs, and I suggest it to everyone no matter what they're symptoms are and whether they are feeling sick or not."

The first thing I needed, according to Dr. Holt, was fiber, which eliminates toxins from the intestinal tract, colon, stomach, liver, gallbladder, and pancreas. Fiber has many benefits; it lowers cholesterol, helps prevent colon cancer, regulates bowels, lessens insomnia and decreases blood pressure.

Fiber, I learned, is not the only thing used for keeping your body's systems clean. Red clover, for example, purifies the blood and cranberry extract cleanses the kidneys. Garlic is also very useful in aiding circulation, building the immune system and killing candida yeast infection.

Another recommendation that Dr. Holt gave me was bee pollen, which has many advantages. He said it can help with weight control, digestion, allergies, energy levels, strength and stamina. It is also helpful in lowering pulse rates, restoring youthful feelings, improving aged skin, and increasing sexual stamina. Of utmost importance to me, however, is its ability to improve recovery power.

Dr. Holt went on to suggest an algae called chlorella. He said it is a good source of high-grade protein and B-complex vitamins, which strengthens the immune system, accelerates the healing of wounds and injuries, protects from toxic pollutants and radiation and, most importantly, stimulates the growth and repair of tissue.

I'd never imagined there were so many natural treatments out there. I wondered why more people didn't know about chromium picolinate, which builds muscle, reduces body fat and stabilizes blood sugar. Or guarana, which increases mental alertness and memory and spirulina, a microalgae which protects the immune system and aids in mineral absorption. Who would have guessed that an herb called goldenseal could protect your body from viral infections, lessen inflammation and regulate menstruation?

I told Dr. Holt that I wanted to know all the benefits of his different recommended remedies. He told me about other things that work together to nourish the body. Ma haung, for example, is an herb which relieves sinus congestion, and ginseng minimizes the effects of stress, strengthens the adrenal glands and enhances learning, productivity and physical stamina. Dr. Holt told me about a purine nucleotide called inosine which increases the amount of oxygen delivered to the cells and fights muscle fatigue – exactly what I needed. He also mentioned cayenne, kola nut, and silmarin.

Minerals are similarly important in that they enable the use of all other nutrients. Dr. Holt informed us that the body must regularly get minerals and trace minerals. He suggested a supplement that consists of all these minerals and trace minerals for me because they enhance normal cellular function and muscular strength, and my tremors were evidence of weak muscles. He also mentioned ginkgo biloba, which strengthens the cardiac and nervous system and increases blood flow and oxygen circulation. "Ginkgo biloba has the ability to cross the blood brain barrier and get into the tiny capillaries of the brain and cleanse them."

In layman's terms, gingko biloba has a significant effect in turning around the aging process in the brain, and it actually increases energy levels, enhances memory, lessens vertigo and headaches, and fights depression. Not only could a nutritional program strengthen the body, it could expand mental capacity.

To assist the body in resisting inflammation, strengthening the arterial system and developing joint flexibility, Dr. Holt suggested Proanthocyanidins. He advised me to take Anthocyanosides, Quercetin, Bromelain, and Hespertin in addition to the old fashioned multi-vitamin.

I left the seminar that night with a new sense of hope and a reinforced sense of belief. You can only imagine my excitement over all these new possibilities! I had, of course, always known that there was something out there that could help me, but now I knew that I had finally found it. I had put my belief in action and I couldn't wait for the results.

As it turns out, I didn't have to wait long at all. The tremors began to disappear and my energy skyrocketed almost immediately after I'd begun the bee pollen, and after only three weeks, I was able to stand without the cane. All over my body, I felt better.

According to Dr. Holt, "There are about ninety nutrients our bodies need on a day to day basis to maintain health. Once you get that into the system, it responds. That's what happened to Dorris. She had done everything possible according to the medical protocol, but not until she added the nutritional component did she see dramatic results. She learned quickly that, even with the finest medical treatment available, your body can still respond positively if you supply it with a balanced nutritional supplementation program."

The improvement that I made from such simple, natural substances amazed me. I was apparently lacking these nutrients and as soon as I started providing them for myself, my entire body responded positively. I would have never been able to do the things I did — like opening Singing Pines and restoring the craft store — if I hadn't been on this program. The supplements restored my energy, however, and I was able to get through my work and do all the things I needed to do.

It was wonderful to be able to work again, since I'd been craving design work for so long. I had so much energy that there were times when I couldn't let myself stop. While most people finish their workdays at five o'clock, I was often still working wildly at the things I had been missing out on. I guess I was making up for lost time!

One thing is for sure: I wouldn't have been doing a quarter of that work if it hadn't been for the nutritional program I was on. Not only did the program give me energy, but it also made my thinking sharper. I made my outlook ten times brighter than it was before, an amazing benefit.

My strength also increased and the better nutrition was the catalyst behind my ability to get on my feet and start walking again. It was as if I was suddenly in a speed recovery mode — everything about me was improving. My joints loosened up almost immediately after I'd begun the program and I was able to do so much more with my hands. It was terrific to suddenly start being able to do all these things that I hadn't previously been able to do. Everyday I gained a new capability and it wasn't long before I could do just about anything I wanted.

I have not faltered from my program since I first tried it; the benefits are too wonderful to give it all up. I truly believe that this program has made the difference in my recovery, which has led me to expand my regimen. It's really very easy and I'm always up for trying something new. In fact, I visited Dr. Holt just the other day to see if he had anything new he could give me.

"I don't have anything to give you, Dorris," he said. "You've got it all."

I know I can always improve my health — always. If I hadn't believed that in the beginning, I wouldn't have worked so hard to go beyond what my doctors were doing for me. It doesn't often matter how determined you are to get the most out of your caregivers or how much you demand of them, but once you've exhausted that resource, you've got to act further. And that's how I came upon Dr. Holt and his wonderful insight to the significance of nutrition. I took the fighting attitude along with me throughout the whole ordeal, which allowed me to discover other possibilities. And it really has made all the difference in the world.

According to Dr. Holt, "Without the proper nutrients, the mental capacity is affected. If you weaken the circuit, anything that comes along will stress a person out even more. But if you strengthen it, it can withstand stress and will play a role in improving attitude as well as physique."

One of my goals is to positively influence at least three people a day, and so far, I believe that I've met that goal. I don't mean that I can turn anyone's world around in line at the grocery store; I simply make a conscientious effort to acknowledge people and therefore encourage them in their quest for improvement.

The simplicity of lifting someone's spirits is thrilling. It's a wonderful thing to know that the person you just talked to is happier now than he was before you spoke. The satisfaction that comes along with helping people, however, was only one of the reasons I vowed to dedicate myself to caring for debilitated people. My major incentive was my faith in God's command. I love God and I know what He wanted from me. Plus, making myself and my contributions available to people in need was an opportunity I could not pass up. Not only would it satisfy God and the sufferers themselves, but it would also satisfy me.

So I went from someone who needed care to someone who gives care, and I think that the decision to do this was one of the best decisions I've ever made. My volunteer work includes counseling those with tragic medical misfortunes, including those stricken with Guillain Barré Syndrome. I celebrate the opportunity to share my story with people every day.

In 1996, I began working as a full-time caregiver for a fifty-year-old woman who had suffered a brain aneurysm three years prior and who was still dealing with the aftereffects. Since she had owned several boutiques, and her story paralleled my own in many ways, I was sure that I could help her.

When I went to visit the Tomlins for the first time, I spoke with Andy, her husband, who told me how discouraged he had become concerning Lois' condition. I gleaned that he was in denial about her situation from what he told me that day.

"Her family left her by herself a lot of the time," Betty recalls. "They didn't know what to do with her."

"First you've got to learn to accept her," I told Andy. "Then you've got to learn to help her help herself."

I told him about my experience in the hospital and in the rehabilitation center, making it clear that had my caregivers not allowed me to do what I needed to do to improve my own condition, I would never have progressed as far as I did.

My contention that friends and families of victims must help them care for themselves was especially prevalent and applicable in the Tomlin household. I recognized that Lois was not receiving the support she needed.

Andy warned me that Lois had no control of her bowels and was constantly messing in her pants and wetting herself.

"I doubt that she really can't control her bowels," I told him. "It sounds to me like she just doesn't think there's a point in trying to control herself. We can change that and I'll make sure that she at least tries to train herself to go to the bathroom."

Lois ran into doors and had no sense of direction. I learned later that this is common in aneurysm patients and is really an effect of their loss of vision. Andy told me that Lois couldn't pick things up with her hands and that her attitude was apathetic; she ignored everything around her and she seemed satisfied living in her own little world. I knew that I couldn't improve her vision or any of her physical abilities, but I could tell just by listening to Andy that Lois needed some encouragement and some incentive to try to make herself better.

"Lois used to stumble into walls all the time and she didn't even care," Betty remembers. "She couldn't gain stability; she didn't know how to move around in this world, but really, she didn't want to learn. She had cuts all over her hands because she wouldn't even try to protect herself. It was definitely an 'I don't care' attitude. It was like she just figured that she'd always be that way and had lost all hope of getting better."

"Don't you want to fix yourself up?" I'd ask her.

"No, no, no," she'd say. "I don't want to."

"You've got to get a life," I told her. "Here you are, you've got a good looking husband with a good job and you won't get out of bed. And even when you're in bed, you're wetting the sheets! Don't you think that he'd like to come in and see you fixed up one day?"

"No. I'm not interested."

Lois' attitude was not unusual. Many people give up on help-ing themselves and settle for a lifetime of being cared for by oth-ers. I was determined to make her realize what she was doing to herself. I'd often hear Andy carrying on in an angry voice late at night, which meant she'd wet the bed.

"What happened last night?" I'd ask her the next morning. "Why was Andy hollering?"

"Because I wet the bed."

"How did you feel when he was hollering at you, Lois?"

"Well, I cried."

"Can you blame him for being angry?" I asked. She shook her head no. "In fact, don't you feel sorry for him?"

"Yes," she whispered.

"Yeah, I do too, but it's not me who can change the situation." I let her think about that for a minute before I said, "You know, he really loves you. If he didn't he wouldn't sleep with you."

"Dorris shamed Lois a lot to make her start caring about the way she was acting," Betty remembers. "And it worked."

If I hadn't, she might never have learned to use the bathroom again. I had to be demanding. A caregiver can't always be posi-tive because if she regards everything the patient does in a posi-tive way, the patient believes the behavior to be acceptable. As a result of being constantly praised, when the patient returns to the real world, she will be met by disappointment when no one else accepts her behavior. It is important for the caregiver to pro-vide realistic feedback. Nothing good can come out of thinking everything's fine. You've got to be motivated to change.

"Lois, I can't motivate you," I would tell her. "You've got to motivate yourself. Once you do that, you can do anything."

It is virtually impossible to motivate anyone just by telling them. The more time I spent with Lois, the more excited I got about helping her. I looked forward to seeing her awaken from the state she'd been in for so long. I didn't know how far I could bring Lois in a physical sense, but I knew I could definitely be a major positive influence for her attitude. I was delighted to be working for something, to have a goal for both Lois and for myself, to be concentrating on something I strongly believed in.

It was almost as if I had returned to that stage in my own recovery when I knew I was getting better and the possibilities of improving were so uplifting. I began to realize that, had I never been stricken with GBS, I would have never had or appreciated the opportunity I had received to make a difference. It wasn't until I met Lois that I was certain that by being stricken with GBS, I was blessed. I was so excited about Lois' improvement, and was willing to do anything for her.

What I did for Lois, I knew, was going to depend greatly on my attitude. During my own recovery process, I had learned how pivotal a caregiver's positive outlook could be in aiding patients in their recovery. I knew that if you feel good, whomever you talk to is going to feel at least a little better when they're with you. It's contagious.

It is important that caregivers know the medications, treatments and therapies, but the attitude a caregiver has toward a patient's recovery is often overlooked and devalued. One of the most crucial duties of the caretaker is becoming acquainted with the patient's individual needs. I knew that Lois needed an attitude adjustment most. And I knew that the best way to do that was to remain positive myself.

"You have to reprogram you mind," I told her after we'd been working together for a few weeks. "Think positive, good, happy thoughts."

"That's easy for you to say," Lois told me. "Everyone who knows you says you have a beautiful attitude. You never get down. I bet you've always been that way."

"No," I said, "I haven't always been that way. I trained myself. I was born into a large family and I was always a part of that family. It's easy to be ignored when you're just one of the fourteen kids, but I figured out pretty quickly that I had be special if I wanted to stand out. So, I became the jolly one; I became the one that everyone came to talk to when they had a problem. And you know what? Plenty of people are able to think positively just by changing the way they think. Anyone can do it. Just laugh. Be kind to people. Always look on the bright side of things. It's easy. And it's fun, too."

Lois seemed to be taking in what I'd said and eventually brightened up. It took some time, but gradually her entire personality changed. She became more caring and aware of the people around her. Although she had been self-absorbed, thinking only of how much help she needed, she soon began to think of all the things that she could do on her own. Her attitude changed and, as it did, she had more incentive to get up and do these things.

As soon as I noticed Lois' attitude changing, I resolved to teach her what I had learned throughout my own time as a patient: patients must be aggressive in their recovery, the focus should always be maximizing future potential and faith is the answer to getting through it all.

I went to the library and researched aneurysms. I learned that her brain damage had affected her motor skills and that those nerves would not heal. However, I discovered that there were hundreds of ways to ensure she could still carry out the essential tasks of life. Everything I read said that, with the proper behavior modification, individuals suffering from brain aneurysms can recover old skills and learn new skills throughout their lives.

Often, when health care professionals say that a patient will not recover, they don't mean that the patient will never be able to function again in daily life, but that the nerves in the brain will never be what they used to be.

Aneurysm sufferers are often discharged when their maximum physical and medical recovery has occurred and, even though the family is usually told they need to live with the patient's remaining disabilities, the behavioral problems are typically pushed aside. The physical limitations are generally clear-cut for patients with brain aneurysms.

Frequently the cognitive and behavioral recovery, which often has the most practical implications, is ignored. The family is left thinking that there is nothing to do about how the patient is acting, but this is not necessarily the case. Therefore, families need to ask which tasks the patient should be able to do independently, which she will need assistance with, and which are more than she can handle. While the physical realities of the patient's condition should always be considered, one should never give up hope for an aneurysm patient's future potential.

Families and caregivers do not generally realize that the extent of an aneurysm patient's rehabilitation depends on them; if they are willing to do everything for the patient, then there is almost no limit to the recovery. However, the patient's abilities are too often either overestimated or underestimated. Expecting too little can definitely retard the patient's recovery. Patience is fundamental in handling the burdens and stress a brain aneurysm sufferer imposes and it is important to do everything possible to find out the implications of the patient's deficits.

One way a caregiver can come to fully understand a patient's limitations is to observe his or her behavior in a variety of circumstances. Does she act different around certain people? Does her behavior change with a different of environment? Does she have more control of her behavior at certain times of day? What are her strengths? What are her weaknesses? What does she do? What doesn't she do? What kind of effect does the mood and the behavior of those around the patient have on her?

All of these circumstances should be considered before developing a plan for aiding the patient in recovery and before trying to teach the patient or modify her behavior. If, for example, the individual is out of control, her behavior must be dealt with before she can begin relearning skills. Helping people regain control over their behavior and their motor skills by getting them into a routine is very beneficial.

Lois was spending her entire day in bed; she had no structural expectations at all. Upon considering all aspects of the situation, caretakers can create a plan that focuses on teaching the patient and family the important skills.

"So," I said to Lois after I'd told her about all the improvement she was capable of making, "you've got a lot of learning to do."

"But the doctors said this was as good as I was going to get," Lois protested.

"They were talking about the tissue in your brain, Lois," I said. "They have no idea how many things you can actually relearn to do."

"Like take my own bath?" she asked.

"Like take your own bath," I smiled, remembering how important that had been for me.

I showed Lois how to get in and out of the tub on her own, wash herself, and wash her hair. "You see? You don't need anyone holding your hand. You can do it. Just take your time."

It wasn't long before Lois could bathe herself. If someone in her situation wants to do something, they can do it. If they don't want to, forget it. Lois had become motivated to improve her appearance and she re-learned to brush her teeth and dress herself.

I had been working with Lois for about seven months when she had surgery to repair the soft spot on her head. I'm not sure what kind of effect that actually had on her physical condition, but she seemed to think it made all the difference in the world — and made a huge difference on her attitude.

I talked to Lois' husband about trying to contact some organizations, but he said he didn't want to seek help.

"I thought that by calling me in you were showing a desire to help Lois," I lectured, staring him down. "Now I see that you don't want help at all. Maybe I should quit and try to find a job with someone who wants help and is willing to do what needs to be done to get it."

Andy quickly changed his mind after that and said he'd try to find some services that could help Lois do things that would make her feel better about herself.

"You need to file for disability," I told him.

"All right, all right," he said, but he didn't say another thing about it for two weeks. Then, one day, he asked me what he could do for Lois.

"You need to go down to Human Services and fill out some forms," I said. "Try to get some insurance to cover her medicine. Then you need to talk to people who can help her. If you don't, you're not going to get anywhere."

Following my advice, he soon found out about all sorts of services. It was as if he'd become a different person, which, in turn, affected Lois. She soon learned the importance of setting small, attainable goals everyday in order to maximize her potential.

"Oh, Dorris," she said to me one day, "I don't think I'll ever be able to cook a meal again. I used to love to cook."

"Of course you can't cook a meal today," I said. "And you're not going to cook a meal tomorrow either. You've got to stop thinking about what you can't do and start thinking about what you can do. And you know what? You'll never be able to bake a potato if you can't learn to tackle this thing step by step! You've really got to start focusing on the things that you can't do right this minute, but that by this time tomorrow you'll be able to do. Work with what you've got. You're lacking the focus that you need. Stop brooding and focus!"

I succeeded in getting Lois to concentrate on one goal at a time, and she finally came to understand that, while she wouldn't eventually recover most details of her former life, this wasn't what was important. She must create a future for herself. After a while, she was able to walk around without stumbling into walls and door frames. She even began to feed herself. Step by step, Lois was able to do things on her own and once she found that she could do so many things independently, her entire personality changed. She wanted to do better.

One day she said, "I'm going to start setting the table." And she started setting the table. From that point, she just moved up. She wanted to do everything!

"Lois Tomlin has regained much of her function," Betty says. "She is really a fine lady. It used to be that she'd just stuff a muffin in her face, but Dorris was always telling her that she couldn't act that way and she stopped."

When I first started working with Lois, all she'd ever wanted to do was sleep. I'd gotten her on a waking schedule and we'd made a little routine; I started getting her up at eight o'clock for her bath, breakfast and medicine and we'd have lunch around noon. Certain times of the day were reserved for therapy, reading, and fun things. Once she was no longer accustomed to sleeping all day, she could always find something new that she wanted to fit into our schedule.

She asked if we could go out, which delighted me, but I made sure that she knew she couldn't go out in public if she couldn't train herself to go to the bathroom.

"Who wants to go out with you?" I said. "Not even your own husband!"

She was determined to go out and now that she knew how to motivate herself, she'd become pretty good at it. It wasn't long until she came into the room and said, "Dorris, I have been using the bathroom since yesterday."

I was so proud of her and I could tell she was proud of herself too. "Come on," I said, "let's go celebrate."

That was a Thursday and from that point on, Thursday was our special day to go out together. I'd take her out for lunch and dinner and we'd go shopping and do whatever else Lois wanted to do that day. Sometimes we'd stay out until ten at night just having a good time.

"Dorris is really good with Lois," Betty says. "They'd go out to eat together and that made Lois so happy because that was something her own family wouldn't even do. Dorris was just amazing with Lois and she always knew how to make her feel good about herself."

I bragged about Lois whenever we went out together. I'd tell the waiters at the restaurants how great she was. "You're looking at one tough cookie," I'd tell them. I know that made Lois happy. You need to hear people say good things about you every once in a while. When other people think that you're good at something, it makes you feel good about yourself.

One of the most important things I did with Lois was to communicate with her. I reminded her over and over again that she had to take control of her life. Even when she'd started improving, I'd tell her that she was in charge. I didn't want her to forget.

"No one is pushing you," I'd tell her. "That's why you have to push yourself. You can do it; it might take you a while, but if you take your time, you can do anything you want."

This kind of encouragement is what people need. It takes a lot of time and effort, but caregivers must be willing to do whatever it takes to motivate their patients.

"How come you have so much faith in me?" Lois asked me one Thursday on our way to lunch.

"Because I have faith in God," I said. "He is my strength and He makes all solutions possible." I was always stressing to Lois the importance of trusting in God. "He'll guide you — I promise."

Lois had a hard time understanding my faith in God because she had never been a religious person. I told her all about what God had taught me and how He had pulled me through my own disease. She was very curious about God and wanted to know how she could start to rely on Him when she hadn't ever believed in Him before. I advised her to join a church to help educate herself and to build a trust in Him. When she told Andy about the idea, however, he scolded her.

"How could you want to go to a church and celebrate the very thing that allowed you to be in the condition you're in now?" he demanded.

"My aneurysm was not His fault, Andy," she said. "It wasn't anyone's fault. It was something that happened and it is something that God is going to help me overcome. If I can deal with that, then you should be able to deal with it too. We're going to church and we're starting this Sunday."

They now go every Sunday and though I'm not sure if Andy's outlook ever changed, I know that Lois' did, and that's what mattered to me. After all, I was Lois' caregiver, not Andy's. But even if Andy had not changed his perspective, he had definitely become more open to God and when I introduced prayer at the dinner table, Andy always wanted to add to the prayer. Not long ago, I think all of our prayers were answered. I know, at least, that Lois' were.

I had spent the day with my son, Michael, who lived in Knoxville then with his wife and son, and I'd told Lois that I would be stopping by her house around five o'clock to check in. When Andy opened the door, I was hit with an array of overwhelming and delicious smells.

I looked down at the newspaper Andy had in his hand. "Did the kitchen get too hot for you?" I asked.

"I wouldn't know if it's hot or not in there," he smiled.

"You mean –"

Just then Lois appeared with a spatula in her hand. She had

an apron on and she was smiling. "How does steak and scalloped potatoes sound to you?" she beamed.

Chills ran through my body as I hurried into the kitchen. "Oh, Lois!" I said, giving her a hug and looking around at the salads, biscuits, steaks and potatoes. "You've done it, haven't you?"

"I did it," she smiled. "I woke up this morning, and I knew I could do it. All it took was believing in myself and that was something that you and God both taught me."

"Well," I said, "aren't you something?"

"Shall we eat?" she asked.

When we'd all settled down around the table, it was Andy who started the prayer.

". . . and God bless the hands that prepared this meal. . . ."

That was the most beautiful meal I had ever sat down to, and it was at that moment that I realized what restoration really was. I had made a difference in someone's life and all it had taken was a little motivation. Just by fostering in Lois a positive attitude and faith in God, I had helped her dreams come true.

That night, I thought back on all the things I'd achieved in my life — all the hard work and effort I had put into my life. I thought about how I loved to keep busy, and I knew that that's exactly what I'd done.

When the doctors first told me I wouldn't be getting out of bed for a long, long time, I had thought that was the worse thing they could have told me. I realized then, however, that Guillain Barré Syndrome had actually been one of the best things that had ever happened to me. It was my biggest challenge and its rewards had been more satisfying than I'd ever imagined was possible. I had gained a whole new perspective, something that I wouldn't give up for the world.

I went to sleep that night with a new comfort. I knew I had accomplished something bigger than anything I'd known before. I had not only restored my own health, but I had restored the well-being of a very special woman. What really comforted and cheered me was knowing I would be waking up to a day full of new challenges and possibilities. And with God's continuing help and blessing, I know I always will.

Appendix I:
SOURCES FOR GUILLAIN BARRÉ SYNDROME
INFORMATION AND SUPPORT

ORGANIZATIONS, ASSOCIATIONS, FOUNDATIONS, INSTITUTIONS, AND SUPPORT GROUPS

GBS FOUNDATION INTERNATIONAL
P.O. Box 262
Wynnewood PA 19096 USA
Telephone: (601) 667-0131
Toll-free telephone (USA only): (800) 732-0999
Facsimile: (610) 667-7036
Email: gbint@ix.netcom.com
Website: http://www.webmast.com/gbs

Support provided: over 143 chapters worldwide assist GBS patients and their families; also a program in which recovered patients visit sick GBS patients.

Newsletter: *The Communicator*. Available in print and online. Current and back issues are both available online and may be accessed through the home page or directly at http://www.webmast.com/gbs/news/index.html

Message/Discussion boards: The Foundation has a total of eight separate discussion boards, each covering a different area of GBS, such as GBS in children or handling the emotional effects of GBS. The discussions are saved and kept in archives for visitors' convenience. The discussion boards can be accessed through the home page or directly at http://www.webmast.com/gbs/hypernews.html

Chat room: The GBS Foundation International provides an active and up-to-date chat room where visitors can communicate directly to other visitors. It may be accessed through the home page or directly, at
http://www.webmast.com/gbs/chat/chat.html

Informative material: The GBS Foundation International offers several guides to the disease for patients, families, parents and caregivers. The site is full of GBS facts and data.

GBS.ORG (an Internet-only organization)
Email: member-services@gbs.org
Website: http://www.gbs.org

Mailing list: GBS.ORG provides an email discussion for patients or loved ones of those suffering from GBS, CIDP and other related syndromes. To subscribe or post messages, go to http://www.gbs.org/mail/lists/ops

Links: The GBS.ORG site has an extensive list of links, including connections to GBS research and history. It also has a page of links to personal stories of people who have been experienced the effects of GBS.

Informative material: The site has many pages of educational data about Guillain Barré Syndrome.

THE NATIONAL ORGANIZATION FOR RARE DISORDERS, INC.(NORD)
100 Route 37
P.O. Box 8923
New Fairfield CT 06812-8923 USA

Telephone: (203) 746-6518
Toll-free telephone: (800) 999-6673
TDD: (203) 746-6927
Facsimile: (203) 746-6481
Email: orphan@nord-rdb.com
Website: http://www.rarediseases.org/

Membership information: To enjoy the benefits that NORD offers, one must join the organization for an annual fee of $30. NORD members also receive a discounted registration fee to NORD's annual conference. If interested in joining, contact NORD Information Services (see above) or visit the membership information page at
http://www.rarediseases.org/help/helpus.htm

Support provided: NORD members benefit from NORD's Patient Assistance Program and their Medication Assistance Program.

Newsletter: *Orphan Disease Update* (ODU). NORD members receive the newsletter three times a year.

Message/discussion board: NORD's Networking Program allows NORD members to communicate with and support each other.

Informative material: Members receive discounted access fees to NORD's Rare Disease Database, which connects to many factual pages about GBS; their Organizational Database, which lists organizations and support available in specific areas; and to their Orphan Drug Designation Database, which has up-to-date information on the latest accomplishments in the research of treating and assisting GBS patients.

NATIONAL INSTITUTES OF HEALTH / NATIONAL INSTITUTE OF NEUROLOGICAL DISORDERS & STROKE (NIH / NINDS)
9000 Rockville Pike
Bethesda, MD 20892 USA
Telephone: (301) 496-5751
Toll-free telephone: (800) 352-9424
Website: (NIH) http://www.nih.gov/
Website: (NINDS) http://www.ninds.nih.gov

Support Provided: The NIH Consensus Program Information Service is offered to answer questions about GBS, available services, and virtually anything else pertaining to health issues. They may be contacted at P.O. Box 2577, Kensington, MD 20891 USA or by toll-free telephone at (800) 644-6627.

Informative Material: Both of the institutes have done significant research, and their sites are full of up-to-date medical information. Some pages to explore:

- The GBS Fact Sheet: http://www.ninds.nih.gov/patients/Disorder/guillain/guillain.htm
- The NIH Consensus Statement Online has a number of articles about GBS and its treatment. This resource may be found at http://odp.od.nih.gov/consensus/cons/conssubj.htm
- "The Utility of Therapeutic Plasmapheresis for Neurological Disorders." The NIH Consensus Statement Online 6.4 (June 1986): 1-7.
- "Intravenous Immunoglobulin: Prevention and Treat ment of Disease." The NIH Consensus Statement Online 8.5 (May 1990): 1-23.

THE NEUROPATHY ASSOCIATION
60 E 42nd Street, Suite 942
New York, NY 10165 USA
Telephone: (212) 692-0662
Toll-free telephone: (800) 247-6968
Website: http://neuropathy.org/index/html

Membership Information: Those who would like to use this organization's services must join first. Membership is free, although financial contributions are welcome.

Message/discussion board: This site offers a newsletter in the form of a bulletin board.

Chat room: The Neuropathy Association has a chat room where GBS patients and their families can go to learn about others like them and to share their experiences with others.

Informative Material: The Association has a number of educational booklets and handbooks available to its members. It also has a directory of support groups and of clinical centers, where GBS patients may locate support groups and medical facilities in their area.

GUILLAIN-BARRÉ SYNDROME SUPPORT GROUP OF THE UNITED KINGDOM
Lincs CC, Council Offices
Eastgate, Sleaford, Lincolnshire NG34 7EB UK
Telephone/facsimile: 01529 304615
Website: http://www.gbs.org.uk/

Membership Information: There are varying levels and costs of membership to the Group. Although some of the benefits of joining — local personal support contacts and access to the help-line, for example — are only available to citizens of the UK and the Republic of Ireland, anyone may join.

Newsletter: *Reaching Out.* Members receive a paper copy of the newsletter three times a year, but it is also posted at the Group's website three times a year. It may either be accessed through the Group menu or by going directly to
http://www.gbs.org.uk/journal.html
Reaching Out has a collection of personal stories, including the following:

♦ Startup, Richard. "The French Connection." *Reaching Out* 27 (Summer 1995): 25.
http://www.adsnet.com/jsteinhi/html/gbs/gbssguk/reachingout.html

♦ Whitehill, John. "Heebee GBS." *Reaching Out* 27 (Summer 1995): 23-4.
http://www.adsnet.com/jsteinhi/html/gbs/gbssguk/reachingout.html

♦ Winer, John. "The Early Years." *Reaching Out* Tenth Anniversary Issue (April 1995): 5.
http://www.adsnet.com/jsteinhi/html/gbs/gbssguk/reachingout.html

Message/discussion board: The Group has a discussion forum, which is available to anyone through the Group's home page or at
http://venus.beseen.com/boardroom/c/26856
Links: This support group provides links to nearly every relevant web page, including sites about Social Security, Medicare/Medicaid, living with disabilities, disability resources, health & wellness and articles about the causes and treatments of GBS. The links can be found at
http://www.gbs.org.uk/links.html.

Informative Material: The Group has many informative pages.
All seven of the Group's published booklets — including a
children's book about GBS and guides for patients, relatives
and friends of GBS patients in Intensive Care, and for the
parents and caretakers of children with GBS — are available
at
        http://www.gbs.org.uk/information.html
This page also has the minutes from the GBS Support Group
of the UK's conferences.

**INFLAMATORY NEUROPATHY SUPPORT GROUP OF
  VICTORIA, INC. (The IN Group)**
        138 b Princess St.
        Kew, Victoria 3101, Australia
        Telephone: +61-3-9853-6443
        Facsimile: +61-3-9853-4150
        Email: ingroup@vicnet.net.au
        Website: http://home.vicnet.net.au/~ingroup/

Membership Information: For an A $5 joining fee and an A $10
annual fee, members of the IN Group are provided with
support and chapter meetings. Most of its services, however,
are available on the Internet.

Informative Material: The IN Group's home page has quite a
few educational pages as well as a support group directory.

Appendix II
INTERNET RESOURCES AND SERVICES CONCERNING
GUILLAIN BARRÉ SYNDROME

WEB SITES

http://www.freeyellow.com/members7/cidpsurvivor/
index.html

♦ Lists doctors, neurologists and rehabilitation centers
according to state.

http://members.tripod.com/~LaurieJeanlinks.html

♦ A comprehensive list of connections to pages with
information about GBS and disabilities.

http://members.aol.com/AdvProsth/MedicalC/
Guillian_Barre_Syndrome.html

♦ Advanced Prosthetics & Orthotics is an informative
and helpful site.

http://neuro-www.mgh.harvard.edu/forum

♦ The Massachusetts General Hospital offers all Internet
users a forum, called the MGH Neurology
WebForum.

http://neuro-www.mgh.harvard.edu/neurowebforum/
neurowebforumold.html

♦ Old discussions that remain available and offer quite
a bit of information.

http://neuro-www.mgh.harvard.edu/interaction$/chat
index.

♦ MGH also offers the Neurology Chat Room.

http://adsnet.com/jsteinhi/html/gbsmain.html

♦ A comprehensive site with links to many different articles.

http://www/emedicine.comEMERG/topic222.htm

♦ For a more clinical and technical look at GBS, take a look at this informative study.

Appendix III
PUBLICATIONS ABOUT GUILLAIN BARRÉ SYNDROME

PUBLICATIONS

Adams, Raymond D., M.D., and Victor Maurice, M.D. *Principles of Neurology*. 4th ed. New York: McGraw-Hill Information Services Company, 1989.

Baier, Sue, and Mary Zimmeth Schomaker. *Bed Number Ten*. Boca Raton, FL: CRC Press, 1989.

Bennett, J. Claude, M.D., and Fred Plum, M.D.. *Cecil Textbook of Medicine*. 20th ed. Orlando: W.B. Saunders Company, 1996.

Berkow, R., et al. *The Merck Manual of Medical Information – Home Edition*. Whitehouse Station: Merck & Co., Inc., 1997.

Brearley, F. R. "A Long Journey Back." *British Medical Journal*, vol. 305, No. 6855 (1992): p. 721.

Cook, Allan R. *Immune System Disorders Sourcebook: Basic Information About Lupus, Multiple Sclerosis, Guillain-Barré Syndrome, Chronic Granulomatous Disease, and more*. Omnigraphic, Inc., 1997.

Coudert, Jo. "I was Trapped in a Useless Body." *Woman's Day*, Vol. 57, No.1 (1993): pp. 56-60.

Donohue, Dr. Paul. "Guillain-Barré: Mystifying, Paralyzing Illness," *St. Louis Dispatch* , August 22, 1997, p. 2E

Hatrick, Gloria. *Masks*. New York: Orchard Books, 1996.

Heller, Joseph, L., and Speed Vogel. *No Laughing Matter*. New York: Donald I. Fine Books, 1995.

Korinthenberg, R., and J. Monting. "Natural History and Treatment Effects in Guillain-Barré Syndrome: a Multicentre Study." *Archives of Disease in Childhood*, vol. 74, no. 4 (1996): pp. 281-287.

McCrum, Robert. *My Year Off*. New York: W.W. Norton, 1998.

Natelson, Benjamin. *Facing and Fighting Fatigue: A Practical Approach.* New Haven: Yale University Press, 1998.

Ouvrier R., and J. McLeod, and J. Pollard. "Chronic Inflammatory Demyelinating Polyradiculoneuropathy." *Peripheral Neuropathy in Childhood*, vol. 5 (1990): pp. 39-49.

Parry, Gareth J. and J. D. Pollard. *Guillain-Barré Syndrome.* New York: Thieme Medical Publishers, 1993.

SEA OATS
PRESS

Write your own book review!

We love to hear from our readers and pass along all the reviews to the author. Tell us what you liked. Tell us what moved you. Tell us what you found most provocative!

Send your reviews to Sea Oats Press, P.O. Box 1898, Mt. Pleasant SC 29465 USA or e-mail them to:

reviews@seaoatspress.com

Thank you!